Every Boy's Handbook

NEWLY REVISED AND TOPICAL

Every Boy's Handbook

HAMLYN

London · New York · Sydney · Toronto

The publishers gratefully acknowledge the help of the British Red Cross Society in preparing pages 196 to 211.

First published 1960
Second impression 1962
First revised edition 1963
Second revised edition 1966
Third revised edition 1968
Fourth revised edition 1970
Fifth revised edition 1972
Sixth revised edition 1973

Published by
THE HAMLYN PUBLISHING GROUP LIMITED
London · New York · Sydney · Toronto

© Copyright Western Publishing Company, Inc. 1960

Printed in Czechoslovakia by Tisk, Brno

ISBN 0 600 33087 7
51080/6

CONTENTS

THE WORLD: USEFUL FACTS AND FIGURES

	Page
The Solar System	14
Land and Water (the Oceans and Continents)	14
Ocean Deeps	15
Great Seas and Lakes	15
Large Islands	16
Great Rivers	18
High Waterfalls	19
Active Volcanoes	19
Principal Mountains	20
Natural Resources of the World	21
Meat and Dairy Produce	21
Sheep and Wool Produce	21
Cereals	21
Tea	22
Coffee	22
Cocoa	22
Sugar	22
Tobacco	22
Cotton	22
Rubber	22
Minerals	23
Fuel	23
Fisheries	23

PEOPLE AND PLACES

The First Men 24
Countries of the World 25
    British Commonwealth 25
    Foreign Countries 28
The World's Largest Cities 32
The World's Tallest Buildings 33
The Seven Wonders of the World 34
Religions of the World 35
Great Dates in History 36
Exploration and Discoveries 40
The United Nations 41
Other Alliances 43
Monarchs of the World 44
The British Commonwealth 45
The Royal Family 45
Kings and Queens of England 46
Kings and Queens of Scotland 48
Royal Salutes 49
The Union Jack 49
The Royal Standard 50
The White, Red and Blue Ensigns 51
British Parliamentary Government 51
Britain's Prime Ministers 52
Some Principal Government Departments 54
How Laws are Made and Who Makes Them . . 55
General Elections—Results 56
Awards and Rewards 57
British Awards for Gallantry 57
British Military Insignia 60
The Duke of Edinburgh's Award 62

PEOPLE AND THE NEW WORLD

Early American Settlements 63
Canada 65
The United States 66
Presidents of the United States 67
Central and South America and the Caribbean . . 69

PEOPLE ON THE MOVE

Man's Fastest Speed 70
Land Speed Records 70
Water Speed Record 70
Great Ships; The Blue Ribands of the Atlantic . . 70
Great Ship Canals 72
Railways 72
British Rail 73
Great Railway Tunnels 74
Principal Railway Gauges of the World 74
Some Principal Wheel Notations for British and
    American Steam Locomotives 75
Navigation 76
Distances by Sea 78
Notable Bridges of the World 79
Distances by Air 80
Local Time throughout the World 80
Aircraft Spotting 83
Car Spotting 84
Signalling 87
Semaphore Code 88
International Code 89
Morse Code 91

PEOPLE AND LANGUAGE

The Development of the Alphabet 93
Principal Languages of the World 93
The English Language 95
Foreign Words and Phrases 97

PEOPLE AND SCIENCE

Brick-making by Machine 104
Cement Manufacture 104
Electric Power 105
Gas Production 105
Glass-making 105
Paper Manufacture 106
Printing 106
Spinning 107
Steel Manufacture 107
Water Supply and Drainage 107
Camera 109
Diesel Engine 109
Internal Combustion Engine 110
Jet Engine 110
   Turbojet 110
   Ramjet 110
Hovercraft 110
Plastics 111
Steam Locomotion 111
Submarine 112
Great Inventions and Discoveries 112
Journeys into Space 114
Nuclear Power 116
Anatomy 118

Weights and Measures 120
Measures and Sizes for Paper and Books 127
Thermometer Readings 128
Roman Numerals 129
Common Formulae 130
Specific Gravity 130
Coefficients of Expansion 130
Boiling Points 131
Speed of Sound 131
Chemical Names of Everyday Substances 131
Table of Elements 132
Chemical Indicators 135
Wind Force 135

PEOPLE AND THE ARTS

Artists, Sculptors, Musicians and Writers of the
Past 137

PEOPLE AND SPORT

Athletics 149
  Running 150
  Field Events 150
  Hurdles 151
Cycling 151
Football 152
Association Football 152
  World Cup Winners 152
  F.A. Cup Winners 153
  Football League Champions 154

Scottish Cup Winners 156
Scottish League Champions 157
Home International Championship 158
Rugby Union 158
International Championship 158
Rugby League 159
Challenge Cup Winners 159
Golf 159
British Open Championship Winners 160
Ryder Cup Competition 160
Walker Cup Competition 161
Lawn Tennis 161
Wimbledon Champions 161
Davis Cup 162
Yachting 163
Cricket 163
Records in Cricket 164
Test Match Results 165
English County Championship 166
Rowing 167
Grand Challenge Cup 168
Diamond Challenge Sculls 168
Oxford and Cambridge Boat Race 169
Cross Country 171
Swimming 171
Walking 172
Ice-Skating 172
Table Tennis 173
Gallery of Sportsmen 174

PEOPLE AND LEISURE

Use of the Road 184
Country Code 188
Map-making and Map-reading 189

Contour Lines	189
Conventional Symbols	190
Map References	190
Camping	192
Tents	194
Youth Hostels	195
First Aid	196
Asphyxia	197
Artificial Respiration	197
Drowning	201
Electric Shock	201
Bleeding or Haemorrhage	201
Shock	203
Unconsciousness	204
Fainting	204
Burns and Scalds	204
Fractures	206
Sprains and Strains	207
Poisoning	207
Snake Bites	208
Sketching and Painting	210
Film Sizes	213
Film Scripting	213
Handicrafts	215
Making Model Railway Scenery	215
Bookbinding	217
Printing from Linocuts	218
Making a Kite	220
Building a Rabbit Hutch	221
Building a Dog Kennel	222
Collecting as a Hobby	224
Stamp Collecting	224
Collecting Match-box Labels	225
Coin Collecting	226
Cigarette-card Collecting	226
Cheese-label Collecting	227

11

Collecting Old Books 228
Collecting Pottery 229
Keeping Pets 230
    Dogs 230
    Cats 232
    Mice 233
    Hamsters 233
    Guinea-pigs 233
    Rabbits 234
    Tortoises 234
    Cage Birds 234
Flowers, Easy-to-Grow 235
    Garden Calendar 238
Judging the Weather 239
Indoor Games 240
    Chess 240
    Draughts 242
    Marbles 242
Secret Codes 243
Personal Record 245
    Weight and Height Charts 246
    Athletics Charts 247

THE WORLD:
USEFUL FACTS AND FIGURES

These tables of sizes, distances, heights and depths, numbers and locations of various things in the world we live in should help in settling many school and family arguments.

The diagram below shows how far the planets are from the Sun in millions of miles:

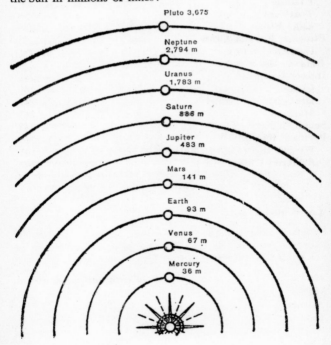

Pluto 3,675

Neptune
2,794 m

Uranus
1,783 m

Saturn
886 m

Jupiter
483 m

Mars
141 m

Earth
93 m

Venus
67 m

Mercury
36 m

13

The Solar System

The sun—the centre of our solar system—has a diameter of about 865,000 miles. The earth is one of nine planets which revolve round the sun. Here are these planets, together with some facts about them:

Planet	Diameter in Miles	One Revolution around Sun (days)	One Rotation on Axis
Mercury	3,008	88	88 days
Venus	7,600	225	not certain
Earth	7,927	365¼	23 h. 56 m.
Mars	4,200	687	24 h. 37 m.
Jupiter	88,439	4,332	9 h. 50 m.
Saturn	75,060	10,759	10 h. 14 m.
Uranus	30,875	30,687	10 h. 49 m.
Neptune	33,000	60,127	15 h. 40 m.
Pluto	3,600	90,400	unknown

The moon—the earth's satellite—has a diameter of 2,160 miles, and it is approximately 239,000 miles away from the earth. Space flights to the moon have revealed no sign of life there, and no definite traces have been discovered on any of the planets—but studies point to possible life of some sort on Mars, probably in the vegetable category.

Land and Water

Much more than half the world's surface is ocean. In fact, the land area is only 56,000,000 square miles out of a total of 197,000,000. The four great oceans are:

Name	Area (millions of sq. miles)
Pacific	64
Atlantic	31.5
Indian	28.35
Arctic	5.5

The six continents are:

Name	Area (millions of sq. miles)
Asia	17
Africa	11.7
North America	9
South America	7
Europe	3.8
Oceania	2.975

Ocean Deeps

Position	Name	Depth (feet)
Mariana Trench	Challenger Deep	37,800
Tonga Trench	—	34,885
Philippine Trench	Galathea Deep	34,580
Kurile Trench	Vityaz Deep	34,045
Japanese Trench	Ramapo Deep	34,035
Kermadec Trench	—	32,788
Guam Trench	—	31,614
Puerto Rico Trench	Milwaukee Deep	30,246
New Britain Trench	Planet Deep	29,987

Great Seas and Lakes

Name and Location	Area (sq. miles)
Mediterranean Sea (Southern Europe, Africa, Asia Minor)	1,100,000
South China Sea (China, East Indies)	960,000
Bering Sea (Alaska, Siberia)	878,000
Caribbean Sea (Central America, West Indies)	750,000
Gulf of Mexico (United States, Mexico)	716,000
Sea of Okhotsk (Siberia)	589,000

Hudson Bay (Canada)	475,000
Sea of Japan (Japan, U.S.S.R., Korea)	389,000
North Sea (North-western Europe)	221,000
Red Sea (Africa, Arabia)	178,000
Caspian Sea (U.S.S.R., Persia)	170,000
Black Sea (U.S.S.R., Turkey, Eastern Europe)	166,000
Baltic Sea (Scandinavia, U.S.S.R.)	163,000
Lake Superior (U.S.A., Canada)	31,820
Lake Victoria (East Central Africa)	26,200
Aral Sea (U.S.S.R.)	24,635
Lake Huron (U.S.A., Canada)	23,010
Lake Michigan (U.S.A.)	22,400
Lake Tanganyika (East Africa)	12,700

Large Islands

Name	Area (sq. miles)
Greenland	840,000
New Guinea	345,000
Borneo	290,000
Madagascar	228,000
Baffin Land (Canada)	197,700
Sumatra	163,000
Great Britain	89,000
Honshu (Japan)	87,500
Ellesmere (Canada)	77,000
Celebes	72,500
South Island (New Zealand)	58,500
Java	48,400
North Island (New Zealand)	44,500
Cuba	44,000
Newfoundland (Canada)	42,750
Luzon (Philippine Islands)	41,000
Iceland	40,000

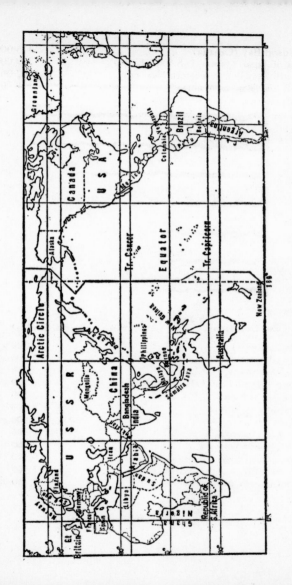

Great Rivers

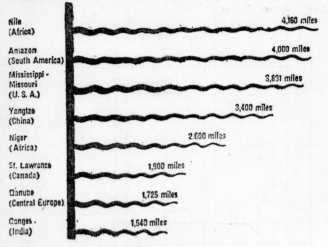

Nile	(Africa)	4,160 miles
Amazon	(South America)	4,000 miles
Mississippi - Missouri	(U. S. A.)	3,891 miles
Yangtze	(China)	3,400 miles
Niger	(Africa)	2,600 miles
St. Lawrence	(Canada)	1,900 miles
Danube	(Central Europe)	1,725 miles
Ganges	(India)	1,540 miles

Other great rivers are:

Name and Location	Length (miles)
Yenisey (Siberia)	3,300
Congo (Africa)	2,900
Lena (Siberia)	2,850
Mekong (South-East Asia, mainland)	2,800
Hwang Ho (China)	2,700
Amur (Siberia, China)	2,700
Ob (U.S.S.R.)	2,600
Mackenzie (Canada)	2,500
Paraná (South America)	2,450
Murray (Australia)	2,310
Volga (U.S.S.R.)	2,300
La Plata (South America)	2,300

18

Yukon (Alaska)	2,000
Rio Grande (Mexico, U.S.A.)	1,800
Sao Francisco (Brazil)	1,800
Euphrates (Iraq)	1,700
Indus (Pakistan)	1,700
Brahmaputra (India)	1,680
Zambezi (Africa)	1,600

High Waterfalls

Name and Location	Height (feet)
Angel Falls (Venezuela)	3,212
Yosemite (California)	2,825
Kukenaam (Venezuela)	2,000
Sutherland (New Zealand)	1,094
Tugela (South Africa)	1,800
Ribbon (California)	1,612
Gavarnie (France)	1,385
Takkakaw (Canada)	1,200
Geissbach (Switzerland)	1,150
Wollomombie (Australia)	1,100
Vettisfos (Norway)	900
Chirombo (East Africa)	880
King Edward VIII (Guyana)	840
Gersoppa (India)	830
Glomach (Scotland)	370
Victoria (Rhodesia, Zambia)	360
Niagara (U.S.A., Canada)	167

Active Volcanoes

Name and Location	Height (feet)
Cotopaxi (Andes, Ecuador)	19,344
Wrangell (Alaska)	14,000
Mauna Loa (Hawaii)	13,675
Erebus (Antarctica)	13,200

Ilamna (Aleutian Islands)	11,000
Etna (Sicily)	10,700
Chillan (Andes, Chile)	10,500
Paricutin (Mexico)	9,000
Asamayama (Japan)	8,200
Heklu (Iceland)	5,100
Vesuvius (Italy)	3,858
Stromboli (Italy)	3,000

Principal Mountains

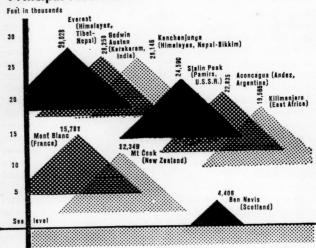

Feet in thousands

Everest (Himalayas, Tibet-Nepal) 29,028
Godwin Austen (Karakaram, India) 28,250
Kanchanjunga (Himalayas, Nepal-Sikkim) 28,146
Stalin Peak (Pamirs, U.S.S.R.) 24,590
Aconcagua (Andes, Argentina) 22,835
Kilimanjaro (East Africa) 19,556
Mont Blanc (France) 15,781
Mt Cook (New Zealand) 12,349
Ben Nevis (Scotland) 4,406

Sea level

Other high mountains are:

Name and Location	Height (feet)
Makalu (Himalayas, Tibet—Nepal)	27,790
Nanga Parbat (Himalayas, India)	26,660

20

Illimani (Andes, Bolivia)	21,185
Chimborazo (Andes, Ecuador)	20,577
McKinley (Alaska)	20,300
Logan (St. Elias, Canada)	19,850
Elbrus (Caucasus, U.S.S.R.)	18,468
St. Elias (St. Elias, Alaska—Canada)	18,008
Popocatapetl (Mexico)	17,883

Natural Resources of the World

The pattern of modern civilisation is based upon what the earth can provide. Lands in which the earth is barren, or the climate too extreme, attract few people unless saleable minerals can be mined; but rich, fertile areas are usually densely populated. In the following paragraphs some of the staple needs of man are listed, with details of the areas in which they are found.

Meat and Dairy Produce. Most peoples of the world are meat eaters, and though cattle for meat can be raised on rough grassland, rich pasture is needed for dairy cattle, the source of milk, from which butter and cheese are made. The great beef-producing countries are the United States, Canada, Argentina and Australia. The major dairying nations are New Zealand, Australia, the United States, Denmark and the Netherlands.

Sheep and Wool Produce. The big sheep-producing countries are Australia, New Zealand, Argentina and Russia. The ideal sheep for economic breeding is a cross between the English strain, raised for its tender meat, and the Merino, of Mediterranean breed, noted for its wool and leather.

Cereals. Man has been developing cereals from the original wild grasses of the world since he first began to cultivate the soil. The principal cereals are wheat, oats, barley, rice, rye and maize. The great wheat areas of the world are Canada, the United States, Argentina, Australia and Eastern Europe. Asia is the source of most of the world's rice.

Tea. Tea is grown mainly in India, China, Ceylon and Japan, with the greatest export trade being carried out by India, which sends millions of pounds in weight every year to the major tea-drinking countries.

Coffee. The coffee plant, which takes five years to grow to a crop-yielding size, is grown mainly in Brazil, Colombia and East Africa.

Cocoa. The cocoa bean was brought back to Europe from Central America in the fifteenth century, by the first explorers. Today the principal growing area is West Africa, which produces enormous quantities every year for making chocolate and cocoa powder.

Sugar. There are two sources of sugar. These are sugar cane and sugar beet. Sugar cane is a tropical plant of which the stems yield a syrupy juice. This is boiled to purify and crystallise it. The juice of the sugar beet, a vegetable grown in temperate climates, is refined in a similar way. The principal sugar cane area is the West Indies.

Tobacco. Grown wild by the natives of North America, tobacco was brought to Europe in the sixteenth century. The main plantations are in the southern United States, but tobacco is also grown extensively in Rhodesia and the Middle East, and to a limited extent in many other areas for local use.

Cotton. Sub-tropical areas are best for cotton production, and the principal cotton countries are the United States, in its southern states, the West Indies, Egypt, India, China and southern Russia.

Rubber. Though some countries now produce much of their rubber by synthetic processes, rubber is still a major source of agricultural revenue for countries bordering the Equator. The main growing area embraces Malaya, to which the original rubber trees were brought from Brazil, and nearby islands of Malaysia and Indonesia. Rubber is collected by cutting narrow grooves in the bark and allowing the natural rubber, or 'latex' to drip into a cup attached to the tree.

Minerals. Mineral ores are the source of the metals man needs, and most of them are found at considerable depth. Open-cast mining is used for surface lodes of minerals, but most mines are deep shafts with underground galleries penetrating hundreds of feet into the heart of the lode. Gold is found mainly in South Africa, Australia and North and South America. Copper and lead are found in every continent, silver in Central and South America and the Far East, and iron in most parts of the world. Uranium, the important metallic element used for atomic energy, is found mainly in the pitchblende deposits of the Congo and Canada.

Fuel. Coal, the source of so many useful by-products, is found extensively and in high quality in Britain, most of Europe and the Eastern seaboard of the United States. Poorer qualities exist in many other parts of the world. The major oil-producing areas are the United States, Canada, Venezuela and the Middle East.

Fisheries. Sea fishing is carried on in all parts of the world, but the areas which produce more than is needed for local consumption are the Grand Banks of Newfoundland, famous for cod, the herring fisheries of Iceland and those stretching southward as far as the Portuguese coast, and the salmon areas of the North Pacific.

PEOPLE AND PLACES

The First Men: Who were the first men? After a succession of ice ages lasting for hundreds of thousands of years, bleak millions of years in which the earth was inhabited by enormous reptiles, further ice ages, and also a long period dominated by early men, who had learned to use primitive tools and clothe themselves, the first true men seem to have emerged about fifty thousand years ago. They were hunters; they used spears and throwing-stones, wore skins and furs, and painted on the walls of their caves—paintings which remain to be seen today in caves in France and Spain.

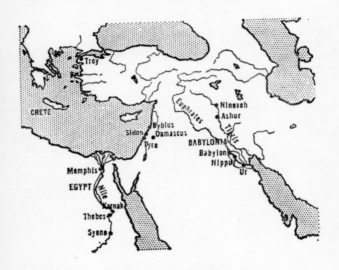

Early Centres of Civilisation

About eight thousand years ago, man had improved to a level at which he made finely polished stone implements, and cultivated fields of corn. Then, about six thousand years ago, came the first civilisations—in the Nile Valley, and in Mesopotamia between the Rivers Tigris and Euphrates. Empires and city-states spread across Arabia, into Turkey and thence to Europe; sailors made their first perilous journeys upon the Mediterranean, taking months of labour and danger to cover distances which a modern liner traverses between sunrise and dusk.

Empire followed empire—Egyptian, Greek, Roman, Chinese—and slowly men grouped themselves by race, religion and way of life into the nations of the present day, while the world's population rose from a few million to the present estimated total of some 3,828,000,000.

Countries of the World. The lists which follow cannot be completely accurate, as not all countries have been fully surveyed and not every area has a census of population, but they are reliable enough for most purposes, based on figures available at the time of going to press.

British Commonwealth

Country	Population in Millions	Capital	Population in Thousands
Europe			
Cyprus	0.633	Nicosia	115,000
United Kingdom	55.5	London	7,379,014
Gibraltar	0.028	Gibraltar	20,000
Malta	0.322	Valletta	15,547
Asia			
Bangladesh	50.8	Dacca	741,000
Brunei	0.130	Brunei	41,000

	Millions		*Thousands*
Hongkong	3.9	Victoria	767,000
India	536.9	Delhi	3,780,423
Malaysia	10.4	Kuala Lumpur	500,000
Singapore	2.9	—	
Sri Lanka	12.2	Colombo	551,200

Africa

Botswana	0.629	Gaborone	18,000
Gambia	0.374	Bathurst	27,809
Ghana	8.5	Accra	633,800
Kenya	10.8	Nairobi	480,000
Lesotho	0.970	Maseru	14,000
Malawi	4.5	Zomba	19,666
Mauritius etc.	0.834	Port Louis	139,681
Nigeria	66.1	Lagos	700,000
Rhodesia	5.1	Salisbury	400,000
Sierra Leone	2.5	Freetown	85,000
Swaziland	0.451	Mbabane	14,000
Tanzania	12.5	Dar-es-Salaam	272,743
Uganda	9.7	Kampala	331,000
Zambia	4	Lusaka	238,000

North America

Canada	21.6	Ottawa	495,535

* Rhodesia declared unilateral independence on 11 November 1965

Central America and West Indies

	Millions		Thousands
Bahamas	0.169	Nassau	112,000
Barbados	0.254	Bridgetown	12,430
Burmuda	0.053	Hamilton	3,000
British Honduras	0.122	Belmopan	3,000
Jamaica	1.8	Kingston	555,110
Trinidad and Tobago	1	Port of Spain	93,950

South America

Falkland Islands	0.002	Stanley	1,052
Guyana	0.714	George Town	168,000

Oceania

Australia	12.7	Canberra	139,800
Fiji	0.524	Suva	54,157
Gilbert and Ellice Islands	0.054	Tarawa	10,616
Nauru	0.007	Nauru	—
New Hebrides	0.086	Vila	5,500
New Zealand	2.8	Wellington	301,300
Papua and New Guinea	2.5	Port Moresby	13,590
Samoa, Western	0.131	Apia	25,000
Tonga	0.087	Nukualofa	9,202

Foreign Countries

Europe

Albania	2	Tirana	50,000
Andorra	0.019	Andorra La Vella	2,500

	Millions		*Thousands*
Austria	7.3	Vienna	1,643,100
Belgium	9.6	Brussels	1,077,035
Bulgaria	8.5	Sofia	868,200
Czechoslovakia	14.4	Prague	1,030,330
Denmark	4.8	Copenhagen	1,199,010
Finland	4.7	Helsinki	526,896
France	50.7	Paris	2,590,000
Germany, West	59.3	Bonn	299,376
Germany, East	15.9	East Berlin	1,200,000
Greece	8.7	Athens	1,852,709
Hungary	10.3	Budapest	2,007,000
Iceland	0.2	Reykjavik	81,354
Irish Republic	2.9	Dublin	568,772
Italy	54.6	Rome	2,778,872
Liechtenstein	0.022	Vaduz	4,070
Luxembourg	0.3	Luxembourg	76,143
Monaco	0.024	Monaco	2,422
Netherlands	13	The Hague	576,160
		Amsterdam	845,821
Norway	3.8	Oslo	486,972
Poland	32.8	Warsaw	1,308,100
Portugal	9.5	Lisbon	820,000
Rumania	20	Bucharest	1,511,388
San Marino	0.019	San Marino	2,000
Spain	33.2	Madrid	3,150,000
Sweden	8	Stockholm	1,306,762
Switzerland	6.2	Berne	166,800
Turkey (Europe)	3.1	Ankara	1,440,779
U.S.S.R. (Europe and Asia)	235.4	Moscow	7,061,000
Vatican City State	0.011	Vatican City	1,000
Yugoslavia	21.5	Belgrade	1,204,000

Asia

	Millions		Thousands
Afghanistan	16.5	Kabul	450,000
Bhutan	0.770	Punakha	
Burma	27.5	Rangoon	1,758,731
China	732	Peking	4,010,000
Indonesia	118	Djakarta	4,750,000
Iran (Persia)	28.4	Tehran	3,150,000
Iraq	9.4	Baghdad	2,696,000
Israel	2.9	Jerusalem	283,000
Japan	103.2	Tokyo	11,403,744
Jordan	2.3	Amman	542,000
Khmer Republic	6.7	Phnom Penh	1,500,000
Korea, North	13.3	Pyongyang	286,000
Korea, South	31.7	Seoul	3,794,959
Laos	2.7	Vientiane	162,297
Lebanon	2.6	Beirut	555,000
Mongolia (Outer)	1.2	Ulan Bator	195,300
Nepal	10.8	Katmandu	224,867
Oman	0.750	Muscat	7,650
Pakistan	42.8	Rawalpindi	340,175
Philippine Islands	39	Manila	2,989,300
Saudi Arabia	7.2	Riyadh	300,000
Syria	6.2	Damascus	599,000
Thailand (Siam)	34.7	Bangkok	1,577,003
Vietnam, North	21.3	Hanoi	800,000
Vietnam, South	17.8	Saigon	2,500,000
Yemen	5	Taiz	20,000
Yemen P.D.R.	1.2	Aden	150,000

Africa

	Millions		Thousands
Afars and Issas Territory	0.081	Jibouti	62,000
Algeria	13.5	Algiers	943,000

29

	Millions		*Thousands*
Angola	5.4	St. Paul de Luanda	346,763
Burundi	3.4	Bujumbura	70,000
Cameroon	5.8	Yaoundé	180,000
Central African Republic	1.5	Bangui	301,793
Chad	3.5	Fort Lamy	45,600
Congo	0.915	Brazzaville	136,000
Dahomey	2.6	Porto Novo	85,000
Equatorial Guinea	0.286	Santa Isabel	9,000
Ethiopia (Abyssinia)	24.7	Addis Ababa	644,190
Gaboon	0.630	Libreville	31,000
Guinea	3.8	Conakry	120,000
Ivory Coast	4.1	Abidjan	400,000
Liberia	1.1	Monrovia	110,000
Libya	1.8	Tripoli	331,947
Madagascar	6.6	Tananarive	364,496
Mali	4.9	Bamako	150,000
Mauritania	1.1	Nouakchott	18,000
Morocco	15.5	Rabat	469,000
Mozambique	7.3	Lourenço Marques	441,363
Niger	4	Niamey	60,000
Portuguese Guinea	0.530	Bissau	6,000
St. Thomé & Principé	0.066	St. Thomé	3,187
Senegal	3.7	Dakar	500,000
Somalia	2.7	Mogadishu	200,000
South Africa	21.2	Pretoria	422,590
		Cape Town	807,211
South West Africa	0.610	Windhoek	60,000

	Millions		Thousands
Spanish Sahara	0.063	Villa Cisneros	250
Sudan	15.3	Khartoum	124,000
Togo	1.8	Lomé	100,000
Tunisia	5.1	Tunis	784,787
Zaire	17.1	Kinshasa	1,300,000
Zambia	4	Lusaka	238,000

Central America and West Indies

Country	Millions	Capital	Thousands
Costa Rica	1.6	San José	205,650
Cuba	8.5	Havana	1,755,360
Dominican Republic	4	Santo Domingo	823,000
Guadeloupe	0.323	Pointe à Pitre	39,000
Guatemala	5	Guatemala	572,900
Haiti	4.7	Port au Prince	300,000
Honduras	2.5	Tegucigalpa	225,000
Martinique	0.332	Fort de France	60,600
Netherlands	0.220	Willemstad	45,000
Nicaragua	1.9	Managua	300,000
Panama	1.4	Panama City	418,000
Puerto Rico	2.7	San Juan	455,421
(El) Salvador	3.3	San Salvador	340,000
Virgin Islands (U.S.)	0.063	Charlotte Amalie	11,000

North America

Country	Millions	Capital	Thousands
Mexico	48.3	Mexico City	8,000,000
United States	203.1	Washington D.C.	2,861,123

South America

	Millions		Thousands
Argentina	23.3	Buenos Aires	7,200,000
Bolivia	4.6	La Paz	553,000
Brazil	93	Brasilia	544,862
Chile	8.8	Santiago	2,100,000
Colombia	22	Bogotá	2,000,000
Ecuador	5.8	Quito	483,847
Guiana, French	0.048	Cayenne	20,000
Paraguay	2.3	Asunción	437,000
Peru	13.6	Lima	2,500,000
Uruguay	2.8	Montevideo	1,173,114
Venezuela	10.3	Caracas	2,064,000

The World's Largest Cities

Name	Population
New York, U.S.A.	11,528,649
Tokyo, Japan	11,403,744
Mexico City, Mexico	8,000,000
London, England	7,379,014
Buenos Aires, Argentina	7,200,000
Moscow, U.S.S.R.	7,061,000
Los Angeles, U.S.A.	7,032,075
Chicago, U.S.A.	6,978,947
Shanghai, China	6,900,000
São Paulo, Brazil	5,901,533
Bombay, India	5,850,000
Cairo, U.A.R	5,126,000
Philadelphia, U.S.A.	4,817,914
Djakarta, Indonesia	4,750,000
Rio de Janeiro, Brazil	4,296,782
Detroit, U.S.A.	4,199,931

Peking, China	4,010,000
Leningrad, U.S.S.R	3,950,000
Seoul, Korea	3,794,959
Delhi, India	3,780,423
Tientsin, China	3,220,000
Berlin, Germany	3,218,256
Madrid, Spain	3,150,000
Tehran, Iran	3,150,000
Calcutta, India	3,141,180

The World's Tallest Buildings

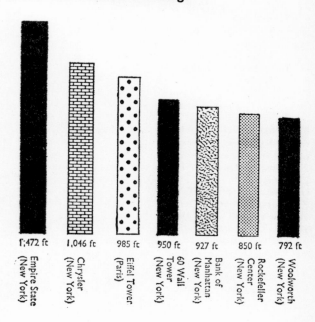

1,472 ft — Empire State (New York)
1,046 ft — Chrysler (New York)
985 ft — Eiffel Tower (Paris)
950 ft — 60 Wall Tower (New York)
927 ft — Bank of Manhattan (New York)
850 ft — Rockefeller Center (New York)
792 ft — Woolworth (New York)

The highest buildings in England are:
Post Office Tower, London—580 ft
Salisbury Cathedral (spire)—404 ft
St. Paul's Cathedral (cross), London—365 ft

The tallest tower in the world is at Ostankino, near Moscow, U.S.S.R. With its television antennae it reaches 1,762 feet. It has a 3-storey restaurant revolving near the top.

The Seven Wonders of the World

It would be a hard task for anyone to name the Seven Wonders of the Modern World, but certainly among the candidates would be nuclear power, the jet engine, television, radar and some of the almost miraculous discoveries of recent years in medicine.

The Seven Wonders of the Ancient World were:

The Pyramids of Egypt, of which the biggest, the Great Pyramid of Cheops, was originally more than 480 feet in height.

The Hanging Gardens of Babylon, near Baghdad. These were terraced gardens, irrigated by means of huge storage tanks on the uppermost terraces.

The Tomb of Mausolus at Halicarnassus, in Asia Minor.

The Temple of Diana (Artemis) at Ephesus, a great marble temple dating from c. 350 B.C.

The Statue of Jupiter (Zeus) at Olympia, built of marble and inlaid with gold about 430 B.C.

The Colossus of Rhodes, a bronze statue (about 105 feet high) with its legs astride the harbour entrance at Rhodes.

The Pharos at Alexandria, the world's first real lighthouse.

Religions of the World

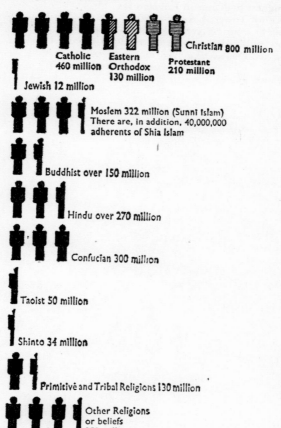

Catholic
460 million

Eastern
Orthodox
130 million

Protestant
210 million

Christian 800 million

Jewish 12 million

Moslem 322 million (Sunni Islam)
There are, in addition, 40,000,000
adherents of Shia Islam

Buddhist over 150 million

Hindu over 270 million

Confucian 300 million

Taoist 50 million

Shinto 34 million

Primitive and Tribal Religions 130 million

Other Religions
or beliefs
350 million

35

Great Dates in History

B.C.

c. 3400	First Egyptian Dynastic Period
c. 2900	The Great Pyramid of Egypt built by Cheops
1300	Phoenicians open up Mediterranean trade
1230	Exodus of the Israelites from Egypt
1190	Fall of Troy
961	Building of the Temple at Jerusalem begun
776	First Olympic Games held in Greece
753	Founding of Rome
490	Greeks defeat Persians at Marathon
488	Death of Buddha
335–23	The campaigns of Alexander the Great
146	Carthage destroyed by Scipio
55	Julius Caesar invades Britain
4	Actual date of the birth of Christ

A.D.

30	Crucifixion
43	Conquest of Britain by Rome begun
70	Destruction of Jerusalem
79	Vesuvius erupts, destroying Pompeii and Herculaneum
122	Building of Hadrian's Wall
407	Romans leave Britain
476	Fall of the Roman Empire in the West
569	Birth of Mohammed in Mecca
711	Moors overrun Spain
732	Moors driven from France
1000	Norsemen reach Labrador
1066	Normans conquer Britain
1095	The Crusades begin
1215	The Magna Carta sealed by King John
1216	First Parliament in England
1271	Beginning of Marco Polo's travels

1338	Hundred Years War begins
1348	The Black Death sweeps Europe
1440	Printing with movable type begun in Germany
1453	Eastern Roman Empire falls to Turks
1455–85	Wars of the Roses
1476	First printing press in England
1492	Columbus discovers America
1492	Moors driven from Spain
1500	Portuguese discover Brazil
1519–22	First voyage round the world, by Magellan
1534	Reformation in England
1536	Dissolution of the monasteries in England
1572	Massacre of St. Bartholomew in France
1577–80	Drake's voyage round the world
1588	Drake defeats Spanish Armada
1605	Gunpowder Plot to blow up English Parliament
1607	First permanent colony established in Virginia
1618–48	Thirty Years War
1620	*Mayflower* colonists land in New England
1642	New Zealand and Tasmania discovered
1665	Great Plague of London
1666	Great Fire of London
1707	Act of Union unites England and Scotland
1715	First Jacobite Rebellion
1745	Second Jacobite Rebellion, 'The Forty-five'
1756	Beginning of Seven Years War
1760	British defeat French in Canada
c. 1760	Beginning of Industrial Revolution
1770	Captain Cook discovers New South Wales
1775–83	American War of Independence
1776	American Declaration of Independence
1789	French Revolution begins
1796	Napoleonic Wars begin
1804	Napoleon becomes Emperor of France
1805	Battle of Trafalgar
1815	Battle of Waterloo

37

1832	First Reform Act in Parliament
1833	Britain abolishes slavery
1840	Introduction of penny post in Britain
1848	Gold discovered in California
1854–56	Crimean War
1857	Indian Mutiny
1861–65	American Civil War
1863	United States abolishes slavery
1867	Dominion of Canada established
1869	Suez Canal opens
1870–71	Franco-Prussian War
1877–78	Russo-Turkish War breaks power of Turkey in Europe
1899–02	Boer War
1903	First successful aeroplane flight, by Wright brothers
1904–05	Russo-Japanese War
1909	Blériot makes first cross-Channel flight
1909	Peary reaches North Pole
1911	Amundsen reaches South Pole
1912	Ocean liner *Titanic* sinks, 1,513 lost
1914	World War I begins
1915	Ocean liner *Lusitania* torpedoed, 1,500 lost
1917	United States enters World War I
1917	Russian Revolution
1918	End of World War I
1919	Alcock and Brown make first non-stop trans-Atlantic flight
1920	First meeting of League of Nations
1922	Mussolini marches on Rome
1924	Death of Lenin
1926	General Strike takes place in Britain
1927	Lindbergh makes first solo flight across Atlantic
1929	Start of the Great Slump
1931	Japan occupies Manchuria
1933	Hitler attains power in Germany

38

1935	Italy invades Ethiopia
1936–39	Civil War in Spain
1937	Japan begins war on China
1938	Germany annexes Austria, Munich Agreement
1939	Outbreak of World War II
1940	Germany invades Denmark, Norway, Netherlands, Belgium and Luxembourg
1940	Dunkirk evacuation. Paris taken by Germans
1940	Battle of Britain
1941	Russia and United States enter World War II
1942	All of France occupied by Germans
1943	Russians halt German advance at Stalingrad
1943	Allies invade Italy
1944	Allies invade France
1945	Germany surrenders. Hitler dies
1945	First atomic bomb dropped on Japan
1945	Japan surrenders
1945	United Nations established
1947	India attains independence
1948	State of Israel proclaimed
1950–53	Korean War.
1953	Conquest of Mount Everest
1956	Suez Canal dispute
1957	Russians launch first space satellites
1959	Russians launch first rocket to reach moon and photograph its far side
1960	Piccard descends 7 miles under the Pacific
1961	First space flight, by Yuri Gagarin
1963	Assassination of President Kennedy
1964	Pope Paul VI visits the Holy Land and becomes first reigning Pope to travel by air
1965	Death of Sir Winston Churchill
1966	River Arno overflows and floods two-thirds of the City of Florence, Italy
1967	China explodes complete H-bomb

1971	Indo-Pakistan conflict. East Pakistan becomes Bangladesh
1971	China admitted to the United Nation

Exploration and Discoveries of the Past Years

1497	East coast of Canada, by John Cabot
1498	Cape route to India, by Vasco de Gama
1498	South America, by Christopher Columbus
1513	Pacific Ocean, by Vasco Nuñez de Balboa
1519	Magellan Strait, by Ferdinand Magellan
1534	St. Lawrence River, by Jacques Cartier
1605–06	Australia, by Willem Jansz
1610	Hudson Bay (Canada), by Henry Hudson
1616	Baffin Bay (Canada), by William Baffin
1642	New Zealand and Tasmania, by Abel Janszoon Tasman
1778	Hawaii, by James Cook
1820	Antarctic mainland, by Edward Bransfield
1855	Victoria Falls, by David Livingstone
1858	Source of the Nile, by John Hanning Speke
1865	Matterhorn summit first reached, by Edward Whymper
1909	North Pole first reached, by Robert E. Peary
1911	South Pole first reached, by Roald Amundsen
1958	American atomic-powered submarine *Nautilus* makes first undersea crossing beneath the North Pole ice cap in 96 hours
1965	Alexei Leonov becomes the first man to walk in space
1966	Russian Space probe achieves first soft landing on the Moon
1969	Neil Armstrong and Edwin Aldrin become the first men to land on the Moon
1971	New peak in American Space Programme reached as U.S. astronauts drive 'Lunar-Rover' across Moon's surface

The United Nations

There has seldom, if ever, been a year without war in some quarter of the globe. In 1944, towards the end of World War II, a conference was held at Washington between statesmen of Britain, China, the Soviet Union and the United States—the four 'Great Powers' on the Allied side in the War—to plan a world-wide organisation of countries pledged to prevent war (successor to the League of Nations). The first full meeting of the United Nations was held in 1945, at San Francisco, and the building of the present headquarters, in New York, was begun soon afterwards. The 126 members of the United Nations are:

Afghanistan
Albania
Algeria
Argentina
Australia
Austria
Barbados
Belgium
Bolivia
Botswana
Brazil
Bulgaria
Burma
Burundi
Byelorussia
Cameroon
Canada
Central African
　Rep.
Chad
Chile
China
Colombia

Congo
Costa Rica
Cuba
Cyprus
Czechoslovakia
Dahomey
Dominican Rep.
Ecuador
Equatorial Guinea
Ethiopia
Fiji
Finland
France
Gaboon
Gambia
Ghana
Greece
Guatemala
Guinea
Guyana
Haiti
Honduras
Hungary

Iceland
India
Indonesia
Iran
Iraq
Irish Republic
Israel
Italy
Ivory Coast
Jamaica
Japan
Jordan
Kenya
Khmer Republic
Kuwait
Laos
Lebanon
Lesotho
Liberia
Libya
Luxembourg
Madagascar
Malawi

Malaysia	Philippines	Togo
Maldive Islands	Poland	Trinidad and
Mali	Portugal	Tobago
Malta	Rumania	Tunisia
Mauritania	Rwanda	Turkey
Mauritius	(El) Salvador	Uganda
Mexico	Saudi Arabia	Ukraine
Mongolia	Senegal	U.S.S.R.
Morocco	Sierra Leone	United Arab Rep.
Nepal	Singapore	United Kingdom
Netherlands	Somalia	United States
New Zealand	South Africa	Upper Volta
Nicaragua	Spain	Uruguay
Niger	Sri Lanka	Venezuela
Nigeria	Sudan	Yemen
Norway	Swaziland	Yemen (P.D.R.)
Pakistan	Sweden	Yugoslavia
Panama	Syria	Zaire
Paraguay	Tanzania	Zambia
Peru	Thailand	

The General Assembly consists of all members. Any important issue brought before it is settled by a two-thirds majority vote; lesser issues require only a simple majority. The Security Council is made up of eleven members and is in continuous session to prevent international disputes. There are five permanent members: United Kingdom, United States, U.S.S.R., France and China. The General Assembly chooses the remaining members, electing them for a period of two years. The Council reaches decisions by a majority of seven votes to four, but in any major issue five of the votes must be those of the permanent members. If any one of these members votes against the majority, this vote is in effect a veto, and no settlement can be reached.

There are four other sections of the United Nations: the Economic and Social Council, the Trusteeship Council, the International Court of Justice and the Secretariat.

The United Nations also runs various agencies, including organisations to provide world banking and trade facilities. Three of these organisations are:

FAO—Food and Agriculture Organisation. This exists to improve nutrition, food production and rural economy.

WHO—World Health Organisation. Its aim is to improve the health of people in all countries through medical research, diet improvement and better hygiene.

UNESCO—United Nations Educational, Scientific and Cultural Organisation. Its purpose is to promote, through education, greater rights and freedoms for all people.

The United Nations Association is a public society which anyone may join. Its purpose is to promote friendship, understanding and co-operation among the peoples of the world and to win support for United Nations work.

Other Alliances

So far, United Nations has had only partial success as a form of 'world government', and nations have still felt it necessary to group themselves for mutual defence. The main groups are as follows:

NATO—North Atlantic Treaty Organisation. This consists of Belgium, Canada, Denmark, France, Greece, Iceland, Italy, Luxembourg, Netherlands, Norway, Portugal, Turkey, United Kingdom, United States and West Germany.

SEATO—South-East Asia Treaty Organisation. The members are Australia, France, New Zealand, Pakistan, Philippines, Thailand, United Kingdom and United States.

Warsaw Pact—This consists of Bulgaria, Czechoslovakia, East Germany, Hungary, Poland, Roumania and U.S.S.R.

Central Treaty Organisation (formerly Baghdad Pact)—This is a Middle East defensive group consisting of Pakistan, Persia, Turkey and the United Kingdom.

EEC (European Economic Community) and *EFTA* (European Free Trade Association) are non-military.

Monarchs of the World

Almost all countries of the world today have a parliamentary system—that is, a council of people elected to rule.

By far the majority of nations have at their head a President, in most cases elected every few years. Those which still have hereditary monarchs are:

Country	Ruler	Came to Throne
Afghanistan	King Mohamed Zahir Shah	1933
Belgium	King Baudouin	1951
Denmark	Queen Margrethe II	1972
Ethiopia	Emperor Haile Selassie	1930
Great Britain	Queen Elizabeth II	1952
Iran	Shah Mohammed Reza Pahlevi	1941
Japan	Emperor Hirohito	1926
Jordan	King Hussein	1952
Liechtenstein	Prince Francis Joseph II	1938
Luxembourg	Grand Duke Jean	1964
Monaco	Prince Rainier	1949
Morocco	King Hassan II	1961
Nepal	Maharajadhiraja Birendra Bir Bikram Shah Deva	1972
Netherlands	Queen Juliana	1948
Norway	King Olav V	1957
Saudi Arabia	King Faisal ibn Abdul Aziz	1964
Sweden	King Gustaf VI Adolf	1950
Thailand	King Bhumibol Adulaydej	1946

Spain has, at present, a Regent—General Francisco Franco—who has announced that the monarchy is to be restored. The future of the Yemen monarchy is doubtful.

The British Commonwealth of Nations

This is a free and equal association of the following nations: The United Kingdom, Australia, Bangladesh, Bahamas, Barbados, Bermuda, Botswana, British Honduras, Brunei, Canada, Cayman, Turks and Caicos Islands, Cyprus, Falkland Islands, Fiji, Gambia, Ghana, Gibraltar, Gilbert and Ellice Islands, Guyana, Hong Kong, India, Jamaica, Kenya, Lesotho, Malawi, Malaysia, Malta, Mauritius, Nauru, New Hebrides, New Zealand, Nigeria, Pitcairn, St Helena, Seychelles, Sierra Leone, Singapore, Solomon Islands, Sri Lanka, Swaziland, Tanzania, Tonga, Trinidad and Tobago, Uganda, Western Samoa, Zambia, Rhodesia. The Queen is Head of the Commonwealth but only remains Head of State in certain instances.

The Royal Family

Her Majesty Queen Elizabeth II succeeded her father, King George VI, at his death on February 6, 1952. Her Coronation was on June 2, 1953. She was born on April 21, 1926, and on November 20, 1947, she married Prince Philip, son of Prince Andrew of Greece. Prince Philip, Duke of Edinburgh, was born on June 10, 1921. Their eldest son, Prince Charles Philip Arthur George, Prince of Wales, the heir to the Throne, was born on November 14, 1948. Their daughter, Princess Anne Elizabeth Alice Louise, was born on August 15, 1950. Their second son, Prince Andrew Albert Christian Edward, was born on February 19, 1960. Their third son, Prince Edward Antony Richard Louis, was born on March 10, 1964.

The other immediate members of the Royal Family are: Queen Elizabeth the Queen Mother, born August 4, 1900, widow of the late King George VI; Princess Margaret Rose, sister of the Queen, born August 21, 1930.

The initial order of succession to the throne is: The Prince of Wales; Prince Andrew; Prince Edward; Princess Anne; Princess Margaret and her son and daughter; The Duke of Gloucester and his son; The Duke of Kent and his sons and daughter; Prince Michael of Kent; Princess Alexandra and her son and daughter.

Kings and Queens of England

Name		Born	Reign	
Saxons and Danes			*From*	*To*
Egbert	c.	775	827	839
Ethelwulf		—	839	858
Ethelbald		—	858	860
Ethelbert		—	858	866
Ethelred I		—	866	871
Alfred the Great	c.	849	871	900
Edward the Elder	c.	870	900	924
Athelstan	c.	895	924	940
Edmund I	c.	921	940	946
Edred	c.	925	946	955
Edwy	c.	943	955	959
Edgar		944	959	975
Edward the Martyr	c.	963	975	978
Ethelred II, the Unready	c.	968	978	1016
Edmund II, Ironside	c.	980	1016	1016
Canute		994	1017	1035
Harold I	c.	1016	1035	1040
Hardicanute	c.	1018	1040	1042
Edward the Confessor	c.	1004	1042	1066
Harold II	c.	1020	1066	1066
House of Normandy				
William I		1027	1066	1087
William II		1057	1087	1100
Henry I		1068	1100	1135
Stephen, Count of Blois		1104	1135	1154

House of Plantagenet

Henry II		1133	1154	1189
Richard I		1157	1189	1199
John		1166	1199	1216
Henry III		1207	1216	1272
Edward I		1239	1272	1307
Edward II		1284	1307	1327
Edward III		1312	1327	1377
Richard II		1367	1377	1399
Henry IV	*Lancaster*	1366	1399	1413
Henry V		1388	1413	1422
Henry VI		1421	1422	1461
Edward IV	*York*	1442	1461	1483
Edward V		1470	1483	1483
Richard III		1452	1483	1485

House of Tudor

Henry VII	1457	1485	1509
Henry VIII	1491	1509	1547
Edward VI	1537	1547	1553
Jane (Lady Jane Grey)—9 days	1537	1553	1553
Mary I	1516	1553	1558
Elizabeth I	1533	1558	1603

House of Stuart

James I (VI of Scotland)	1566	1603	1625
Charles I	1600	1625	1649

Commonwealth created May 19, 1649, causing Interregnum

Oliver Cromwell (Lord Protector)	1599	1653	1658
Richard Cromwell (Lord Protector)	1626	1658	1659

House of Stuart (Restoration)

Charles II		1630	1660	1685
James II		1633	1685	1688
William III	*joint sovereigns*	1650	1689	1702
Mary II		1662		1694
Anne		1665	1702	1714

House of Hanover

George I	1660	1714	1727
George II	1683	1727	1760
George III	1738	1760	1820
George IV	1762	1820	1830
William IV	1765	1830	1837
Victoria	1819	1837	1901

House of Saxe-Coburg

Edward VII	1841	1901	1910

House of Windsor

George V	1865	1910	1936
Edward VIII—325 days	1894	1936	1936
George VI	1895	1936	1952
Elizabeth II	1926	1952	—

Kings and Queens of Scotland

Name	Reign	
	From	To
Malcolm III (Canmore)	1057	1093
Donald I	1093	1094
Duncan II	1094	1094
Donald I (restored)	1094	1097
Edgar	1097	1107
Alexander I	1107	1124
David I	1124	1153
Malcolm IV (the Maiden)	1153	1165
William I (the Lion)	1165	1214
Alexander II	1214	1249
Alexander III	1249	1286
Margaret (Maid of Norway)	1286	1290
John Baliol	1292	1296
Robert I (Bruce)	1306	1329
David II	1329	1371
Robert II (Stewart)	1371	1390

Robert III	1390	1406
James I	1406	1437
James II	1437	1460
James III	1460	1488
James IV	1488	1513
James V	1513	1542
Mary (Queen of Scots)	1542	1567
James VI (became James I of England in 1603)	1567	1625

Royal Salutes

A Royal Salute of sixty-two guns is fired at the Tower of London each year on the anniversaries of the Queen's Birth, Accession to the Throne and Coronation. Forty-one guns are fired when the Queen opens or dissolves Parliament in person, when she passes through London in procession, and on the birth of a Royal child.

The Union Jack

The Union Jack is a flag composed of three crosses. These are the crosses of St. Andrew (white on blue), St. Patrick (red on white) and St. George (red on white). The first two are diagonal, the third vertical and horizontal. At the time it was adopted (1606) the flag contained only the crosses of St. George and St. Andrew, as it signified the accession of James VI of Scotland to the English Throne as James I. The cross of St. Patrick (Ireland) was introduced when the Act of Union came into force in the year 1800. The flag is flown on government and public buildings in the United Kingdom, England, Scotland or Greater London (according to the event) on a number of Royal anniversaries and other important occasions, such as Commonwealth Day (May 24) and Remembrance Sunday (nearest to November 11), and at the special command of Her Majesty. It is flown at half-mast as a mark of respect when the death takes place of the Sovereign, Prime Minister and other important personages at home or abroad.

| Blue | Yellow | Red |

The Royal Standard

The Royal Standard is the personal flag of the Queen and is flown only on buildings in which the Queen is actually present, never when Her Majesty is passing in procession. It is divided into four quarters. In the first and fourth are the three lions passant of England; in the second appears the lion rampant of Scotland; in the third, the harp of Ireland.

The White, Red and Blue Ensigns

The White Ensign, bearing the cross of St. George on a white background, with the Union Jack filling the upper corner nearest the flagstaff, is the flag of the Royal Navy and the Royal Yacht Squadron.

The Red Ensign (the Red Duster) is a red flag with the Union Jack filling the upper corner nearest the flagstaff. It is flown by British merchant vessels.

The Blue Ensign is a blue flag with the Union Jack in the upper corner nearest the flagstaff. It is flown by the Royal Naval Reserve and by certain selected yacht clubs.

British Parliamentary Government

The Queen, though Head of the British Commonwealth, takes a purely formal part in government, which is carried on in each Commonwealth nation by a Prime Minister, and/ or President, and his Cabinet, usually drawn from the membership of its Parliament. The Queen opens Parliament in Britain by making a speech from the Throne in the House of Lords, and the same ceremony has been carried out by Her Majesty in Commonwealth nations—though, as she is normally resident in Britain, this is usually the task of the Governor-General, who is the Queen's representative in those countries that recognise Her Majesty as Head of State. Other Commonwealth countries (Republics, etc.) have a High Commissioner in place of a Governor-General.

The method of government—usually parliamentary— varies considerably from one Commonwealth country to the next, but the pattern is generally based upon that of Britain, where the Cabinet consists of about seventeen Ministers. The head of the Cabinet is the Prime Minister, whose appointment is made personally by the Queen on the recommendation of 'elder statesmen'—senior politicians with a long record in public life.

51

Britain's Prime Ministers and changes of administration

Date	Name	Party
1721	Sir Robert Walpole	Whig
1742	Earl of Wilmington	Whig
1743	Henry Pelham	Whig
1754	Duke of Newcastle	Whig
1756	Duke of Devonshire	Whig
1757	Duke of Newcastle	Whig
1761	Earl of Bute	Tory
1763	George Grenville	Whig
1765	Marquess of Rockingham	Whig
1766	Earl of Chatham	Whig
1767	Duke of Grafton	Whig
1770	Lord North	Tory
1782	Marquess of Rockingham	Whig
1782	Earl of Shelburne	Whig
1783	Duke of Portland	Coalition
1783	William Pitt	Tory
1801	Henry Addington	Tory
1804	William Pitt	Tory
1806	Lord Grenville	Whig
1807	Duke of Portland	Tory
1809	Spender Perceval	Tory
1812	Earl of Liverpool	Tory
1827	George Canning	Tory
1827	Viscount Goderich	Tory
1828	Duke of Wellington	Tory
1830	Earl Grey	Whig
1834	Viscount Melbourne	Whig
1834	Sir Robert Peel	Tory
1835	Viscount Melbourne	Whig
1841	Sir Robert Peel	Tory
1846	Lord John Russel	Whig
1852	Earl of Derby	Tory
1852	Earl of Aberdeen	Peelite

1855	Viscount Palmerston	Liberal
1858	Earl of Derby	Conservative
1859	Viscount Palmerston	Liberal
1865	Lord John Russell	Liberal
1866	Earl of Derby	Conservative
1868	Benjamin Disraeli	Conservative
1868	William E. Gladstone	Liberal
1874	Benjamin Disraeli	Conservative
1880	William E. Gladstone	Liberal
1885	Marquess of Salisbury	Conservative
1886	William E. Gladstone	Liberal
1886	Marquess of Salisbury	Conservative
1892	William E. Gladstone	Liberal
1894	Earl of Rosebery	Liberal
1895	Marquess of Salisbury	Conservative
1902	A. J. Balfour	Conservative
1905	Sir H. Campbell-Bannerman	Liberal
1908	Herbert Asquith	Liberal
1915	Herbert Asquith	Coalition
1916	David Lloyd George	Coalition
1922	Andrew Bonar Law	Conservative
1923	Stanley Baldwin	Conservative
1924	J. Ramsay MacDonald	Labour
1924	Stanley Baldwin	Conservative
1929	J. Ramsay MacDonald	Labour
1931	J. Ramsay MacDonald	Coalition
1935	Stanley Baldwin	Coalition
1937	Neville Chamberlain	Coalition
1940	Winston Churchill	Coalition
1945	Clement R. Attlee	Labour
1951	Sir Winston Churchill	Conservative
1955	Sir Anthony Eden	Conservative
1957	Harold Macmillan	Conservative
1963	Sir Alec Douglas-Home	Conservative
1964	Harold Wilson	Labour
1970	Edward Heath	Conservative

Some Principal Government Departments of the United Kingdom

Agriculture and Fisheries. Farming, fishing, the maintenance and improvement of food supplies, and animal health. (Minister of Agriculture, Fisheries and Food)

Defence. The overall responsibility for national defence by the co-ordination of air, naval and military preparedness. (Secretary of State for Defence)

Education and Science. The organisation of the State educational system, from primary schools to universities and adult education. (Secretary of State for Education and Science)

Employment. All matters concerned with employment. (Secretary of State for Employment)

Environment. All matters concerning the environment. (Secretary of State for the Environment)

Foreign and Commonwealth Affairs. All matters relating to foreign and Commonwealth countries. (Secretary of State for Foreign and Commonwealth Affairs)

Health and Social Security. The running of the National Health Service. All matters concerning medicine, nursing, hospitals and public hygiene. The administration of insurance, family allowances, widows' and retirement pensions. (Secretary of State for Social Services)

Home Office. Law enforcement. The control of fire, police, prison and immigration services. (Secretary of State for the Home Department)

Housing and Construction. Housing and new towns, control of the use of land, and relations between central and local government. (Minister for Housing and Construction)

Posts and Telecommunications. The operation of the postal collection and delivery services, and telephone and telegraph services, collection of national insurance payments and certain revenues, payment of allowances and pensions, and operation of the National Savings Scheme. (Minister of Posts and Telecommunications)

Scottish Office. All matters of particular concern to Scotland. (Secretary of State for Scotland)

Trade and Industry. Matters affecting British industry and trade, other than those handled by the Ministers of Agriculture, Fisheries and Food, and the Environment. (Secretary of State for Trade and Industry, and President of the Board of Trade)

Transport Industries. Road, rail and sea transport of people and goods. (Minister for Transport Industries)

Treasury. All matters relating to finance and the national budget. (Prime Minister and First Lord of the Treasury and the Chancellor of the Exchequer)

Welsh Office. All matters of particular concern to Wales. (Secretary of State for Wales)

How Laws are Made and Who Makes Them

New laws are discussed and voted upon in the two Houses of Parliament. The House of Lords, presided over by the Lord High Chancellor, has a membership of about one thousand, comprising Royal princes, archbishops, dukes, marquesses, earls, viscounts, bishops, barons, life peers and law lords. The House of Commons, directed by the Speaker, is an elected assembly of six hundred and thirty men and women who are paid an annual salary for attendance. Each represents a constituency (area of the country) which elected him or her by majority vote at the last General Election, or a later By-election caused by the death or retirement of the previous representative. The normal span of a Parliament is five years, though at any time the Queen may, upon the advice of the Prime Minister, dissolve Parliament and proclaim a General Election. It is also possible that the Government may be defeated in the House of Commons on a major issue. It may then be forced to resign, in which case either the next strongest party forms a government, or a new election is sought. All but a handful of the Members of the House of Commons belong to one or other of the main political parties, and after a General Election it is the party with most Members which forms the Government. At certain times of national crisis, two or more parties may unite to form a Coalition Government.

New Laws start as Bills. Any Member of the Lords or Commons can introduce a Bill, though the majority are brought in by the Government, based on its plans as outlined in the Queen's Speech at the Opening of Parliament. The Bill has to pass through three Readings before it is considered to be agreed by the House of Commons. It then goes forward to the House of Lords. If it is a Financial Bill, the House of Lords must pass it without making any changes, but the Lords can reject any other Bill; after the lapse of a year, the Lords' rejection does not prevent its being passed and forwarded to the Queen for her Assent.

General Elections—Results

Party	Votes	Seats in the House of Commons
1964		
Labour	12,205,581	317
Conservative*	11,980,783	303
Liberal	3,101,103	9
Others (including Communist)	368,682	0
1966		
Labour	13,064,951	363

Conservative*	11,418,433	253
Liberal	2,327,533	12
Others	452,689	1
(including Communist)		(Republican Labour)

1970

Conservative*	13,144,692	330
Labour	12,179,166	287
Liberal	2,177,638	6
Others		
(including Communist)	903,311	7

The Speaker (non-party and non-voting) was also elected.
* *and associated parties*

Awards and Rewards

Most countries reward their great men and women with decorations for gallantry in war, or titles for loyal and useful service in times of peace. In Britain, for example, a brilliant discovery by a scientist may gain him a knighthood or baronetcy.

The greatest international awards are the Nobel Prizes. Dr Alfred Nobel, the Swedish scientist who invented dynamite, left well over a million pounds to provide a fund which would award annual prizes of nearly £ 14,000 to the most deserving man or woman working in each of the following activities: Physics Research, Chemistry Research, Physiology and Medicine, Literature, Promotion of Peace.

British Awards for Gallantry

The Victoria Cross. This was first awarded in June, 1856, and the bronze crosses were made from guns captured from the enemy during the Crimean War. The last of this metal

Victoria Cross

George Cross

Distinguished
Service Order

Distinguished
Conduct Medal

Distinguished
Service Cross

George
Medal

Military
Cross

Air Force
Cross

Distinguished
Flying Cross

Distinguished
Flying Medal

Air Force
Medal

Albert
Medal

Military
Medal

Queen's
Police Medal

 Red   Blue   Purple   Claret

was used up in 1942, and since then the crosses have been made of gun-metal from the Royal Mint. The cross is worn before all other decorations. It is one-and-a-half inches across, and bears the Royal Crown surmounted by a lion. It carries the inscription 'For Valour', and has a claret ribbon. The cross is awarded to anybody serving with or under the command of the armed forces who performs an act of great bravery in the presence of the enemy.

The George Cross. First awarded in 1940, this decoration is a silver cross with a dark blue ribbon. The inscription is 'For Gallantry', and the design shows St George and the Dragon. It is awarded to civilians, and it is only given to members of the fighting services for the greatest gallantry in circumstances in which military awards could not normally be granted.

The Distinguished Service Order is awarded to officers of the armed services or the Merchant Navy.

The Distinguished Service Cross is for Royal Naval officers below the rank of captain, and warrant officers.

The Military Cross is awarded to Army and Colonial Army captains, lieutenants and regimental sergeant-majors.

The Distinguished Flying Cross is for Royal Air Force and Fleet Air Arm officers and warrant officers for gallantry while flying in operations against the enemy.

The Air Force Cross is for acts of gallantry in the air but not in operations against the enemy.

The Albert Medal is given for gallantry in saving life at sea or on land.

The Distinguished Conduct Medal is awarded to warrant officers, non-commissioned officers and men of the Army and Royal Air Force.

The Conspicuous Gallantry Medal is for warrant officers and men of the Royal Navy, Merchant Navy or Royal Air Force.

The George Medal is given for acts of gallantry.

The Queen's Police and Fire Services Medal for gallantry.

The Edward Medal is for heroic acts by miners or quarrymen, or by those engaged in rescuing them.

The Distinguished Service Medal is for chief petty officers, petty officers and men of the Royal Navy, and equivalent ranks in the Royal Marines and Merchant Navy.

The Military Medal is awarded to warrant officers, non-commissioned officers and men and women of the Army.

The Distinguished Flying Medal is awarded for gallantry to non-commissioned officers and men of the Royal Air Force while flying in operations against the enemy.

British Military Insignia

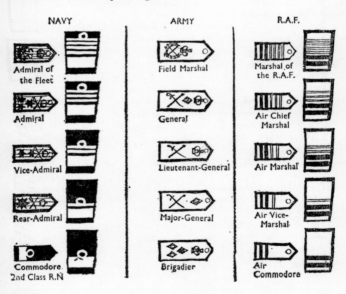

NAVY	ARMY	R.A.F.
Admiral of the Fleet	Field Marshal	Marshal of the R.A.F.
Admiral	General	Air Chief Marshal
Vice-Admiral	Lieutenant-General	Air Marshal
Rear-Admiral	Major-General	Air Vice-Marshal
Commodore 2nd Class R.N.	Brigadier	Air Commodore

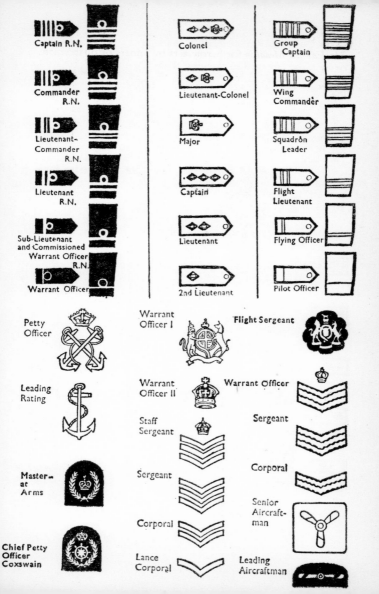

Captain R.N.

Commander R.N.

Lieutenant-Commander R.N.

Lieutenant R.N.

Sub-Lieutenant and Commissioned Warrant Officer R.N.

Warrant Officer

Colonel

Lieutenant-Colonel

Major

Captain

Lieutenant

2nd Lieutenant

Group Captain

Wing Commander

Squadron Leader

Flight Lieutenant

Flying Officer

Pilot Officer

Petty Officer

Leading Rating

Master-at-Arms

Chief Petty Officer Coxswain

Warrant Officer I

Warrant Officer II

Staff Sergeant

Sergeant

Corporal

Lance Corporal

Flight Sergeant

Warrant Officer

Sergeant

Corporal

Senior Aircraftman

Leading Aircraftman

The Duke of Edinburgh's Award

This is a scheme begun in 1956 for young people between the ages of fifteen and eighteen, to encourage development of character. There are three awards—bronze, silver and gold—for attaining certain standards over a wide range of activities. To gain an award a boy must demonstrate his ability in self-reliance by planning and carrying out cross-country journeys, his fitness by reaching certain athletic standards, his competence in carrying out first aid and camp work, and his progress in his own chosen hobby. Boys intending to take part can obtain details through their schools or youth clubs.

PEOPLE AND
THE NEW WORLD

Early American Settlements

It was in the fifteenth century that the people of Europe began to look for new lands in which they could find broader commercial scope and, later, personal freedom. The American continent had been discovered by Scandinavian seamen five centuries earlier, but no settlements had remained. Voyagers such as Christopher Columbus believed that a westward course would lead them to India, and so when they reached America they called it the Indies.

Settlement in North, South and Central America was rapid. The Spanish and Portuguese colonised the South, the French and English the North. The struggles for power lasted for more than a century before the present boundaries and governments became settled. Britain at one time controlled all of eastern North America, but this direct government from London came to an end with the establishment of the United States as an independent nation during the War of 1775—1783 and the creation of Canada as a Dominion in 1867.

The development of the New World has been man's greatest achievement, for it required a mass migration of people, over a long period, from Europe and Africa to colonise such an enormous area as North America, which had previously been inhabited only by wandering indigenous tribes, wrongly called 'Indians'. Two hundred years ago the United States was a group of British colonies on the Eastern seaboard, still struggling to win a living from a new

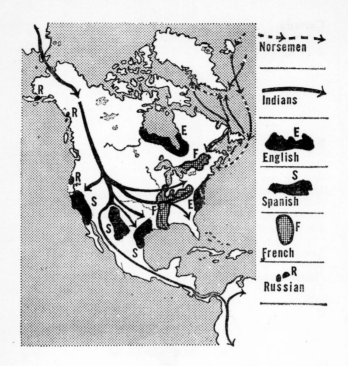

country, to cut back the forests and plough the land in order to grow crops which would pay for their import from Europe. Today the United States is the wealthiest nation in the world, with one of the highest standards of living. In material assets, it has more cars, telephones, television sets, radios, etc., per thousand of its population than any other nation. Canada, though slower to develop, has raised its standard of living in very much the same way.

64

Canada

Canada is made up of twelve provinces and territories listed below with their dates of admission as provinces:

Province or Territory	Capital	Date of Admission	Population
Alberta	Edmonton	1905	1,600,000
British Columbia	Victoria	1871	2,014,000
Manitoba	Winnipeg	1870	988,000
New Brunswick	Fredericton	1867	616,788
Newfoundland	St. John's	1949	517,000
Nova Scotia	Halifax	1867	770,000
Ontario	Toronto	1867	7,637,000
Prince Edward Island	Charlottetown	1873	110,000
Quebec	Quebec	1867	6,003,000
Saskatchewan	Regina	1905	942,000
North-West Territories	Ottawa	—	34,500
Yukon Territory	Whitehorse	—	22,000

Ottawa is also the capital of all of Canada.

Growth of the United States in Population

= 5 million people

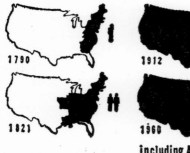

including Alaska & Hawaii

The United States

The United States is made up of fifty States and the Federal District of Columbia (Washington, D.C.). These are:

Name and Abbreviation	Capital	Date of Admission to the Union
Alabama (Ala.)	Montgomery	1819
Alaska	Juneau	1959
Arizona (Ariz.)	Phoenix	1912
Arkansas (Ark.)	Little Rock	1836
California (Calif.)	Sacramento	1850
Colorado (Colo.)	Denver	1876
Connecticut (Conn.)	Hartford	1788*
Delaware (Del.)	Dover	1787*
District of Columbia (D.C.)	Washington	1791
Florida (Fla.)	Tallahassee	1845
Georgia (Ga.)	Atlanta	1788*
Hawaii	Honolulu	1959
Idaho	Boise	1890
Illinois (Ill.)	Springfield	1818
Indiana (Ind.)	Indianopolis	1816
Iowa (Ia.)	Des Moines	1846
Kansas (Kans.)	Topeka	1861
Kentucky (Ky.)	Frankfort	1792
Louisiana (La.)	Baton Rouge	1812
Maine (Me.)	Augusta	1820
Maryland (Md.)	Annapolis	1788*
Massachusetts (Mass.)	Boston	1788*
Michigan (Mich.)	Lansing	1837
Minnesota (Minn.)	St. Paul	1858
Mississippi (Miss.)	Jackson	1817
Missouri (Mo.)	Jefferson City	1821
Montana (Mont.)	Helena	1889

Nebraska (Nebr.)	Lincoln	**1867**
Nevada (Nev.)	Carson City	**1864**
New Hampshire (N.H.)	Concord	**1788***
New Jersey (N.J.)	Trenton	**1787***
New Mexico (N. Mex.)	Santa Fé	**1912**
New York (N.Y.)	Albany	**1788***
North Carolina (N.C.)	Raleigh	**1789***
North Dakota (N. Dak.)	Bismarck	**1889**
Ohio	Columbus	**1803**
Oklahoma (Okla.)	Oklahoma City	**1907**
Oregon (Oreg.)	Salem	**1859**
Pennsylvania (Pa.)	Harrisburg	**1787***
Rhode Island (R.I.)	Providence	**1790***
South Carolina (S.C.)	Columbia	**1788***
South Dakota (S. Dak.)	Pierre	**1889**
Tennessee (Tenn.)	Nashville	**1796**
Texas (Tex.)	Austin	**1845**
Utah	Salt Lake City	**1896**
Vermont (Vt.)	Montpelier	**1791**
Virginia (Va.)	Richmond	**1788***
Washington (Wash.)	Olympia	**1889**
West Virginia (W.Va.)	Charleston	**1863**
Wisconsin (Wis.)	Madison	**1848**
Wyoming (Wyo.)	Cheyenne	**1890**

* *One of the Thirteen Original States*

Presidents of the United States

In the American system of government the President combines his Presidential powers with many of those held by a Prime Minister under a system such as that in most Commonwealth countries, and is, therefore, a man of great personal influence during his term of office. The Presidents of the United States have been as follows overleaf...

George Washington	Federalist	1789
John Adams	Federalist	1797
Thomas Jefferson	Republican	1801
James Madison	Republican	1809
James Monroe	Republican	1817
John Quincy Adams	Republican	1825
Andrew Jackson	Democratic	1829
Martin Van Buren	Democratic	1837
William Henry Harrison	Whig	1841
John Tyler	Whig	1841
James Knox Polk	Democratic	1845
Zachary Taylor	Whig	1849
Millard Fillmore	Whig	1850
Franklin Pierce	Democratic	1853
James Buchanan	Democratic	1857
Abraham Lincoln	Republican	1861
Andrew Johnson	Republican	1865
Ulysses Simpson Grant	Republican	1869
Rutherford Birchard Hayes	Republican	1877
James Abram Garfield	Republican	1881
Chester Alan Arthur	Republican	1881
Grover Cleveland	Democratic	1885 and 1893
Benjamin Harrison	Republican	1889
William McKinley	Republican	1897
Theodore Roosevelt	Republican	1901
William Howard Taft	Republican	1909
Woodrow Wilson	Democratic	1913
Warren Gamaliel Harding	Republican	1921
Calvin Coolidge	Republican	1923
Herbert Clark Hoover	Republican	1929
Franklin Delano Roosevelt	Democratic	1933
Harry S. Truman	Democratic	1945
Dwight D. Eisenhower	Republican	1953
John Fitzgerald Kennedy	Democratic	1961
Lyndon B. Johnson	Democratic	1963
Richard M. Nixon	Republican	1969

Central and South America and the Caribbean

The countries of Central and South America are independent, with the exception of British Honduras, French Guiana and Surinam (Netherlands Guiana), and a number of island dependencies. They are:—

Name	Date of Gaining Independence
Argentina	1816
Bolivia	1825
Brazil	1822
Chile	1818
Colombia	1819
Costa Rica	1821
Cuba	1902
Dominican Republic	1821
Ecuador	1822
Guatemala	1821
Guyana*	1966
Haiti	1804
Honduras	1821
Jamaica*	1962
Mexico	1810
Nicaragua	1821
Panama	1903
Paraguay	1811
Peru	1821
(El) Salvador	1821
Trinidad and Tobago*	1962
Uruguay	1825
Venezuela	1821

* *Member of the British Commonwealth of Nations*

PEOPLE ON THE MOVE

Two hundred years ago man's fastest way of travelling or sending a message was on horseback. The following information shows how much the picture has changed.

Man's Fastest Speed

The American research rocket craft 'X-15' has continually broken the world speed record for winged aircraft in flights at high altitudes to test, mainly, the heat resistance of metals. On June 23, 1961, U.S.A.F. Major Robert White flew the 'X-15' at 3,603 m.p.h. This, of course, cannot compare with the speeds of astronauts. In orbital flight, for example, United States astronauts have reached 24,791 m.p.h.

Land Speed Records

In November, 1965, two land speed records were set up by Americans at Bonneville Salt Flats, U.S.A.—Robert Summers, in a wheel-drive car, at 418.504 m.p.h.; Craig Breedlove, in a jet-driven car, at 613.995 m.p.h.

Water Speed Record

The water speed record of 328 m.p.h., set up on Coniston Water in Lancashire in January, 1967, stands to the credit of the late Donald Campbell, who was the son of Sir Malcolm Campbell, holder of both land and water speed records in the nineteen-thirties.

Great Ships; The Blue Riband of the Atlantic

The fifteenth-century voyages of Columbus to America took many weeks of hardship; today it takes five days to cross from Britain to the United States and would take less than four days at maximum speeds. For nearly a century there has been keen competition between the great seafaring nations for the Blue Riband—the Championship of the Atlantic. The following table shows the progress of the Blue Riband since 1900.

Year	Direction	Ship	Tonnage	Time		
				d.	h.	m.
1903	West-East	Deutschland (German)	16,502	5.5	—	—
1904	West-East	Kaiser Wilhelm II (German)	19,361	5	8	16
1909	East-West	Lusitania (British)	31,550	4	11	42
1909	East-West	Mauretania (British)	30,696	4	10	41
1929	West-East	Bremen (German)	51,650	4	14	30
1929	East-West	Bremen		4	18	17
1930	East-West	Europa (German)	51,656	4	17	6
1933	East-West	Bremen		4	17	43
1933	East-West	Rex (Italian)	50,000	4	13	58
1934	West-East	Empress of Britain (British)	42,348	4	6	58
1935	East-West	Normandie (French)	80,000	4	3	2
1936	East-West	Queen Mary (British)	81,237	4	0	27
1936	West-East	Queen Mary		3	23	57
1937	East-West	Normandie		3	23	2
1938	East-West	Queen Mary		3	21	45
1938	West-East	Queen Mary		3	20	42
1952	West-East	United States (American)	51,500	3	10	40
1952	East-West	United States		3	12	12

The largest ocean liners in the world are the FRANCE (French: 66,348 tons), QUEEN ELIZABETH 2 (British: 65,863 tons), RAFFAELLO (Italian: 45,933 tons), MICHEL-ANGELO (Italian: 45,911 tons), CANBERRA (British: 44,807 tons), ORIANA (British: 41,910 tons), UNITED STATES (U.S.A.: 38,216 tons), ROTTERDAM (Netherlands: 37,783 tons), NIEUW AMSTERDAM (Netherlands: 36,982 tons), and WINDSOR CASTLE (British: 36,123 tons).

Great Ship Canals

	Year Opened	Length (miles)	Width (feet)	Depth (feet)
Gota (Sweden)	1832	115	47	10
Suez (Egypt)	1869	100	197	34
Kiel (Germany)	1895	61	150	45
Panama (Panama)	1914	50.5	300	45
Elbe (Germany)	1900	41	72	10
Manchester (England)	1894	35.5	120	28–30
Welland (Canada)*	1887	26.75	200	25
Princess Juliana (Netherlands)	1935	20	52	16
Amsterdam (Netherlands)	1876	16.5	88	23
Corinth (Greece)	1893	4	72	26.25

* *Reconstructed, and reopened 1931*

Railways

The first steam railway locomotive was tried out in 1804 at Merthyr Tydfil in Wales, but the first to be successful was the famous *Puffing Billy,* installed at Wylam Colliery near Newcastle-on-Tyne in 1813, and in use until 1872 when it was bought by the government to be kept as a museum piece. In 1825 the Stockton and Darlington Railway was opened for goods traffic using a locomotive supplied by George Stephenson. Stephenson was the successful winner four years later, with his locomotive *Rocket,* of a competition to choose the locomotive for the Liverpool and Manchester Railway. Stephenson's locomotive drew thirty passengers at up to twenty-nine miles an hour. Today there are probably nearly a million miles of railway in the world, and the French have a locomotive capable of speeds over 200 miles an hour.

British Rail

The following are a few interesting facts and figures about British Rail:—

Largest station area	Clapham Junction (34½ acres)
Largest number of platforms	Waterloo (21)
Largest platform	Manchester (Victoria & Exhange) (2,194 feet)
Highest track altitude	Druimuachdar (1,484 feet above sea level)
Lowest point of railway	Severn Tunnel (144 feet below sea level)
Longest straight stretch	Between Selby and Hull (Yorks.) (18 miles)
Longest stretch of continuous four-track main line	St. Pancras to Glendon North Junction, Kettering (74 miles, 78 chains)
Longest bridge	Tay Bridge (2 miles, 364 yards)
Longest tunnel	Severn Tunnel (4 miles, 628 yards)

The five Regions of British Rail are:

London Midland Region (formerly the London Midland and Scottish Company in the areas of England and Wales)
Western Region (formerly the Great Western Railway)
Southern Region (formerly the Southern Railway)
Eastern Region (formerly the Southern and North Eastern areas of the London and North Eastern Railway)
Scottish Region (formerly the Scottish areas of the London Midland and Scottish and the London and North Eastern Railways).

Great Railway Tunnels

Name	Location	Length (miles)
London Transport (Northern Line, City Branch)	London	17½
Simplon	Switzerland—Italy	12¼
Apennine	Italy	11½
St Gotthard	Switzerland	9¼
Lötschberg	Switzerland	9
Mont Cenis	France—Italy	8½
Cascade	South Dakota, U.S.A.	7¾
Arlberg	Austria	6⅓
Moffat	Colorado, U.S.A.	6
Shimizu	Japan	6
Kvineshei	Norway	5¾
Rimutaka	New Zealand	5⅓
Otira	New Zealand	5¼
Tauern	Austria	5¼
Connaught	British Columbia, Canada	5
Ste Marie-aux-Mines	France	4½
Severn	England	4⅓

Principal Railway Gauges of the World

Gauge	Where in Use
5 ft 6 in.	Spain, Portugal, Argentina, Chile, India, Ceylon, Pakistan
5 ft 3 in.	Ireland, Brazil, Victoria (Australia), South Australia
5 ft 0 in.	U.S.S.R.
4 ft 8½ in.	Great Britain, Europe (except Portugal, Spain, U.S.S.R.), Canada, U.S.A., Mexico, Uruguay, Peru, North Africa, Middle East, Egypt, Turkey, Australian Commonwealth, New South Wales (Australia), China, Korea

74

3 ft 6 in.	South and Western Australia, Queensland (Australia), New Zealand, Tasmania, South Africa, East and West Africa, Indonesia, Sudan, Sweden, Norway, Japan, Newfoundland (Canada), Costa Rica, Nicaragua, Honduras
3 ft 5¼ in.	Algeria, Jordan, Syria
3 ft 3⅜ in.	South America, East and West Africa, Malaya, Burma, Thailand, Indo-China, Indonesia
3 ft 0 in.	Ireland, South America, El Salvador, Guatemala, Panama
2 ft 11 in.	Sweden
2 ft 6 in.	India, Ceylon
2 ft 0 in.	South America, India, Pakistan, Wales

Some Principal Wheel Notations for British and American Steam Locomotives

Wheels	Notation	Type
oO	2–2–0	Planet
oOo	2–2–2	Jenny Lind
ooOo	4–2–2	Bicycle
OO	0–4–0	Four-wheel Switch
OOo	0–4–2	—
ooOO	4–4–0	American
oOOo	2–4–2	Columbia
ooOOo	4–4–2	Atlantic
OOoo	0–4–4	Four-coupled
OOooo	0–4–6	Four-coupled
ooOOoo	4–4–4	Jubilee
OOO	0–6–0	Six-wheel Switch
OOOo	0–6–2	—
oOOO	2–6–0	Mogul
ooOOO	4–6–0	Ten-wheel
oOOOo	2–6–2	Prairie

ooOOOo	4–6–2	Pacific
OOOoo	0–6–4	Six-coupled
OOOooo	0–6–6	Six-coupled
oOOOoo	2–6–4	Adriatic
ooOOOoo	4–6–4	Hudson
OOOO	0–8–0	Eight-wheel
oOOOO	2–8–0	Consolidation
ooOOOO	4–8–0	Twelve-wheel
oOOOOo	2–8–2	Mikado
ooOOOOo	4–8–2	Mountain
oOOOOoo	2–8–4	Berkshire
ooOOOOoo	4–8–4	Northern
oOOOOO	2–10–0	Decapod
ooOOOOO	4–10–0	Mastodon
oOOOOOo	2–10–2	Santa Fé
ooOOOOOo	4–10–2	Overland
oOOOOOoo	2–10–4	Texas
ooOOOOOOo	4–12–2	Union Pacific
oOOOOOOo	2–6–6–2	—

Navigation

How does a ship find its way across thousands of miles of ocean and yet arrive at the harbour mouth as unerringly as a car steered home to its garage?

A nautical chart looks much like a road map, except that the roads are 'sea lanes', with lightships, buoys, shoals and sandbanks instead of towns, railways, church towers and hilltops. And, of course, the lines of latitude and longitude are clearly marked.

Before leaving port, the ship's navigator marks out his route on the chart. This chart is generally on what is known as 'Mercator's Projection', which means all the lines of longitude, or meridians, run parallel, whereas in reality, of course, they meet at the Poles. The compass points to *Magnetic* North, which is a variable number of miles away from *True* North, so that in working out the course the navigator must allow for this variation. This may be ten or more degrees—and it is found on the 'compass rose', a compass diagram printed on the chart at frequent intervals, or published in nautical tables.

For a course due East—90°—with a variation of 10° East the *Magnetic* course would be 80°. But before setting this for the helmsman, the navigator checks his deviation card—a note of any errors in the compass when it was last tested. Suppose the deviation is 2° West; then that would have to be *added* to the figure of 80° to give the final compass course that the helmsman will follow.

But the helm alone won't keep a ship on its course, so at sea the navigator uses the chronometer and sextant to check at regular intervals. The time of the ship's clocks is changed as it travels East or West of the Greenwich Meridian (0° longitude), and the difference between the ship's clocks (showing local time) and the chronometer (showing Greenwich time) tells the navigator his longitude. This is a simple calculation: there are 360° of longitude, and the earth turns once on its axis in every 24 hours; 360 divided by 24 gives us 15—which means one hour of 'sun's progress' equals 15°. When it is noon at Greenwich, it is 1 p.m. if you are 15° East, and 11 a.m. if you are 15° West.

Latitude is checked by a sextant. This is a device for measuring angles, and as we know from generations of navigation just where the sun ought to be at a given latitude on any particular occasion, and where each of the principal stars should appear at night, a check of the angle between the sun, moon or stars and the horizon provides a figure which need only be looked up in a standard book of tables carried by every ship.

This, of course, is the method out at sea, where no landmarks are available to help in navigation. Along the coast the task of the officer on the bridge is much easier, for he can take bearings of lighthouses, church spires, prominent hilltops and other easily recognisable points marked on his chart. Where the bearings intersect is the ship's position.

Radio is another important aid to the navigator. He can take bearings from radio beacons—fixed points which send out radio signals in the same way that a lighthouse transmits intermittent beams of light. And, most important of all, he can use radar, a British invention which makes it possible for the navigator to know where ships, wrecks, buoys and other dangers are in relation to his own vessel. The radar set sends out ultra-short-wave impulses in all directions; any of these striking an object sends back an echo to the set, and this appears as a bright dot on the monitor screen.

Distances by Sea

Using normal shipping routes, these are the distances of some of the world's principal seaports from Britain.

Name	Distance (miles)	Name	Distance (miles)
Alexandria (Egypt)	2,950	Mombasa (Kenya)	5,980
Basra (Iraq)	6,053	Montreal (Canada)	2,760
Bombay (India)	5,910	New York (U.S.A.)	3,118
Cape Town (South Africa)	5,978	Rangoon (Burma)	7,590
Copenhagen (Denmark)	683	Rio de Janeiro (Brazil)	5,030
Gothenburg (Sweden)	584	Sydney (Australia)	12,201
Hong Kong	9,743	Tunis (North Africa)	2,050
Karachi (Pakistan)	5,730	Valparaiso (Chile)	7,207
Manila (Philippine Islands)	9,650	Wellington (New Zealand)	11,096
Marseilles (France)	1,833	Yokohama (Japan)	11,536

Notable Bridges of the World

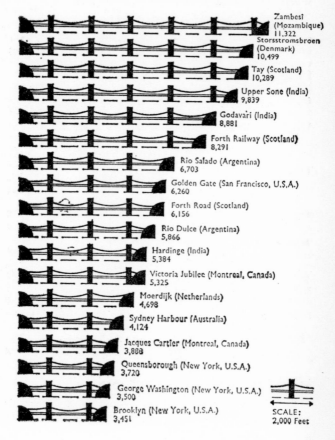

Zambesi (Mozambique) 11,322

Storsstromsbroen (Denmark) 10,499

Tay (Scotland) 10,289

Upper Sone (India) 9,839

Godavari (India) 8,881

Forth Railway (Scotland) 8,291

Rio Salado (Argentina) 6,703

Golden Gate (San Francisco, U.S.A.) 6,260

Forth Road (Scotland) 6,156

Rio Dulce (Argentina) 5,866

Hardinge (India) 5,384

Victoria Jubilee (Montreal, Canada) 5,325

Moerdijk (Netherlands) 4,698

Sydney Harbour (Australia) 4,124

Jacques Cartier (Montreal, Canada) 3,888

Queensborough (New York, U.S.A.) 3,720

George Washington (New York, U.S.A.) 3,500

Brooklyn (New York, U.S.A.) 3,451

SCALE: 2,000 Feet

Distances by Air

These are the distances of principal world cities from London by air, using the shortest routes.

Name	Distance (miles)	Name	Distance (miles)
Aden	4,104	Madrid (Spain)	775
Amsterdam (Netherlands)	231	Melbourne (Australia)	11,934
Athens (Greece)	1,501	Montreal (Canada)	3,310
Baghdad (Iraq)	3,063	Moscow (U.S.S.R.)	1,549
Berlin (Germany)	593	Munich (Germany)	588
Bombay (India)	4,901	Nairobi (Kenya)	4,429
Brussels (Belgium)	218	New York (U.S.A.)	3,500
Chicago (U.S.A.)	4,127	Nicosia (Cyprus)	2,028
Colombo (Ceylon)	5,854	Oslo (Norway)	722
Copenhagen (Denmark)	609	Paris (France)	215
Djakarta (Indonesia)	8,337	Prague (Czechoslovakia)	670
Geneva (Switzerland)	468	Rome (Italy)	908
Gibraltar	1,085	San Francisco (U.S.A.)	6,169
Hong Kong	8,102	Singapore	7,678
Johannesburg (South Africa)	6,227	Stockholm (Sweden)	899
Karachi (Pakistan)	4,428	Teheran (Persia)	3,419
Kingston (Jamaica)	5,207	Tel Aviv (Israel)	2,230
Kuala Lumpur (Malaya)	7,883	Tokyo (Japan)	10,066
Lagos (Nigeria)	3,401	Venice (Italy)	703
Lisbon (Portugal)	972	Vienna (Austria)	791
		Warsaw (Poland)	914

Local Time throughout the World

As you travel eastwards from Greenwich, the longitude time (see under **Navigation**) is one hour later for every

15°; to the west it is an hour earlier. But for convenience local clocks don't always show the correct longitude time, otherwise travellers inside even a quite small country would be constantly confused. In Britain, all clocks show Greenwich Mean Time. Only in big countries such as Canada, the U.S.S.R., the United States, etc., are time zones necessary.

Here are the local times in various big cities when it is noon in London:

City	Time	City	Time
Adelaide (Australia)	8.30 p.m.	Caracas (Venezuela)	6.30 a.m.
Algiers	noon	Chicago (U.S.A.)	5 a.m.
Amsterdam (Netherlands)	noon	Colombo (Ceylon)	4.30 p.m.
Ankara (Turkey)	1 p.m.	Copenhagen (Denmark)	noon
Athens (Greece)	1 p.m.	Dakar (Senegal)	10 a.m.
Belgrade (Yugoslavia)	noon	Djakarta (Indonesia)	7 p.m.
Berlin (Germany)	noon	Edinburgh (Scotland)	noon
Bombay (India)	4.30 p.m.	Gibraltar	noon
Boston (U.S.A.)	6 a.m.	Guatemala City (Guatemala)	5 a.m.
Brussels (Belgium)	noon	Guayaquil (Ecuador)	6 a.m.
Bucharest (Roumania)	1 p.m.	Halifax (Canada)	7 a.m.
Budapest (Hungary)	noon	Havana (Cuba)	6 a.m.
Buenos Aires (Argentina)	8 a.m.	Helsinki (Finland)	1 p.m.
Cairo (Egypt)	1 p.m.	Hobart (Tasmania)	9 p.m.
Calcutta (India)	4.30 p.m.	Hong Kong	7 p.m.
Canton (China)	7 p.m.	Honolulu (U.S.A.)	1 p.m.
Cape Town (South Africa)	1 p.m.	Johannesburg (South Africa)	1 p.m.

81

Karachi		Peking (China)	7 p.m.
(Pakistan)	4 p.m.	Perth (Australia)	7 p.m.
Kingston	6 a.m.	Prague	
(Jamaica)		(Czechoslovakia)	noon
La Paz (Bolivia)	7 a.m.	Rangoon	
Leningrad		(Burma)	5.30 p.m.
(U.S.S.R.)	2 p.m.	Reykjavik	
Leopoldville		(Iceland)	10 a.m.
(Congo)	noon	Rio de Janeiro	
Lima (Peru)	6 a.m.	(Brazil)	8 a.m.
Lisbon (Portugal)	noon	Rome (Italy)	noon
Madrid (Spain)	noon	San Francisco	
Manila (Philippine		(U.S.A.)	3 a.m.
Islands)	7 p.m.	Santiago (Chile)	7 a.m.
Mecca		Shanghai (China)	7 p.m.
(Saudi Arabia)	2 p.m.	Singapore	6.30 p.m.
Melbourne		Sofia (Bulgaria)	1 p.m.
(Australia)	9 p.m.	Stockholm	
Mexico City		(Sweden)	noon
(Mexico)	5 a.m.	Sydney	
Montevideo		(Australia)	9 p.m.
(Uruguay)	8 a.m.	Teheran (Persia)	2.30 p.m.
Montreal		Tel Aviv (Israel)	1 p.m.
(Canada)	6 a.m.	Tokyo (Japan)	8 p.m.
Moscow		Toronto (Canada)	6 a.m.
(U.S.S.R.)	2 p.m.	Vancouver	
Nairobi (Kenya)	2 p.m.	(Canada)	3 a.m.
New Orleans		Vienna (Austria)	noon
(U.S.A.)	5 a.m.	Warsaw (Poland)	noon
New York		Wellington	
(U.S.A.)	6 a.m.	(New Zealand)	11 p.m.
Oslo (Norway)	noon	Winnipeg	
Panama City		(Canada)	5 a.m.
(Panama)	6 a.m.	Zürich	
Paris (France)	noon	(Switzerland)	noon

Aircraft Spotting

When travelling by air you can easily tell the country of origin of other aircraft you see around you by their registration marks. All planes other than military aircraft carry two groups of letters on the wings. The first group indicates the country of origin, thus 'G-ABC' would be a British aircraft with the distinguishing letters 'ABC'. Many of the national markings are as follows:

Marking	Country	Marking	Country
AN	Nicaragua	HH	Haiti
AP	Pakistan	HI	Dominican Republic
B	Formosa		
CC	Chile	HK	Colombia
CCCP	U.S.S.R.	HL	Korea
CF	Canada	HP	Panama
CN	Morocco	HS	Thailand
CP	Bolivia	HZ	Saudi Arabia
CR	Portuguese Colonies	I	Italy
		JA	Japan
CS	Portugal	JY	Jordan
CU	Cuba	LG	Guatemala
CX	Uruguay	LN	Norway
CZ	Monaco	LV	Argentina
D	Germany	LX	Luxembourg
EC	Spain	LZ	Bulgaria
EI	Ireland	N	U.S.A.
EL	Liberia	OB	Peru
EP	Persia	OD	Lebanon
ET	Ethiopia	OE	Austria
F	France	OH	Finland
G	Great Britain	OK	Czechoslovakia
HA	Hungary	OO	Belgium
HB	Switzerland	OY	Denmark
HC	Ecuador	PH	Netherlands

PI	Philippine Islands	XA, XB, XC	Mexico
PJ	Netherlands Antilles	XH	Honduras
PK	Indonesia	XT	China
PP, PT	Brazil	XY, XZ	Burma
PZ	Surinam	YA	Afghanistan
SA	Libya	YE	Yemen
SE	Sweden	YI	Iraq
SN	Sudan	YJ	New Hebrides
SP	Poland	YK	Syria
SU	Egypt	YR	Rumania
SX	Greece	YS	(El) Salvador
TC	Turkey	YU	Yugoslavia
TF	Iceland	YV	Venezuela
TI	Costa Rica	ZA	Albania
VH	Australia	ZK	New Zealand
VQ, VP, VR	British Colonies and British Protectorates	ZP	Paraguay
		ZS	South Africa
		3W	Vietnam
		4R	Sri Lanka
VT	India	4X	Israel

Car Spotting

If you're keen on car spotting, carry your Handbook with you when you're on a journey. The following tables will help you to identify cars from overseas, for cars travelling outside their countries of registration carry special identification letters as well as their normal registration plates. The national markings are:

Marking	Country	Marking	Country
A	Austria	BDS	Barbados*
ADN	Aden State*	BG	Bulgaria
AL	Albania	BH	British Honduras*
AND	Andorra		
AUS	Australia,* Norfolk Islands*	BL	Basutoland (Lesotho)*
B	Belgium	BP	Bechuanaland (Botswana)*

BR	Brazil	EAT	Tanganyika (now Tanzania)*
BRG	British Guiana (Guyana)*		
BRN	Bahrain*	EAU	Uganda*
BRU	Brunei*	EAZ	Zanzibar (now Tanzania)
BS	Bahamas*		
BUR	Burma*	EC	Ecuador
C	Cuba	ET	Egypt (now U. A. R.)
CDN	Canada		
CGO	Congo (Leopoldville)	F	France, and French Overseas departments
CH	Switzerland		
CI	Ivory Coast		
CL	Ceylon (Sri Lanka)	FL	Liechtenstein
CNB	North Borneo, Labuan (now Sabah-Malaysia)*	GB	Great Britain and Northern Ireland*
		GBA	Alderney*
		GBG	Guernsey*
		GBJ	Jersey*
CO	Colombia	GBM	Isle of Man*
CR	Costa Rica	GBY	Malta,* Gozo*
ČS	Czechoslovakia	GBZ	Gibraltar
CY	Cyprus*	GCA	Guatemala
D	Germany (Federal Republic)	GH	Ghana*
		GR	Greece, Crete, Dodecanese Islands
DK	Denmark, Faroe Islands		
		H	Hungary
DOM	Dominican Republic	HK	Hong Kong*
		I	Italy, Sardinia, Sicily
DY	Dahomey		
DZ	Algeria	IL	Israel
E	Spain, Balearic Islands, Canary Islands, Spanish Guinea and Spanish Sahara	IND	India*
		IR	Iran (Persia)
		IRL	Republic of Ireland (Eire)*
		IRQ	Iraq
EAK	Kenya*	IS	Iceland*

J	Japan*		Portuguese West Africa (Angola), São João Baptista de Ajuda, St Thomé and Principé Islands
JA	Jamaica,* Cayman Islands,* Turks and Caicos Islands*		
JOR	Jordan	PA	Panama
K	Cambodia (Khmer Republic)	PAK	Pakistan*
		PE	Peru
KWT	Kuwait	PI	Philippine Islands
L	Luxembourg	PL	Poland
LAO	Laos	PTM	Malaysia (Malaya)*
LT	Libya		
MA	Morocco	PY	Paraguay
MC	Monaco	R	Rumania
MEX	Mexico	RA	Argentina
MS	Mauritius*	RCA	Central African Republic
N	Norway		
NA	Netherlands Antilles	RCB	Republic of the Congo (Zaïre)
NGN	West Irian (formerly Netherlands New Guinea)	RCH	Chile
		RH	Haiti
		RI	Indonesia
NIC	Nicaragua	RIM	Islamic Republic of Mauretania
NIG	Niger*		
NL	Netherlands (Holland)	RL	Lebanon
NZ	New Zealand*	RM	Malagasy Republic
P	Portugal, The Azores, Cape Verde Islands, Madeira, Mozambique, Portuguese Guinea, Portuguese Timor,	RMM	Mali
		RNR	Zambia (formerly) Northern Rhodesia)*
		RNY	Malawi* (formerly Nyasaland)

RSM	San Marino	TG	Togo
RSR	Rhodesia*	TN	Tunisia
RWA	Republic of Ruanda and Kingdom of Burundi (formerly Ruanda-Urundi)	TR	Turkey
		TT	Togo
		U	Uruguay
		USA	United States of America
S	Sweden	V	Vatican City State
SA	Saar	VN	Vietnam
SD	Swaziland*	WAG	Gambia*
SF	Finland	WAL	Sierra Leone*
SGP	Singapore*	WAN	Nigeria*
SK	Sarawak*	WD	Dominica (Windward Islands)*
SME	Surinam (formerly Dutch Guinea)		
		WG	Grenada (Windward Islands)*
SN	Republic of Senegal	WL	St. Lucia (Windward Islands)*
SU	Union of Soviet Socialist Republics		
		WS	Western Samoa*
SUD	Sudan	WV	St. Vincent (Windward Islands)*
SWA	South West Africa		
SY	Seychelles*	YU	Yugoslavia
SYR	Syria	YV	Venezuela
T	Thailand (Siam)*	ZA	Republic of South Africa*
TD	Trinidad and Tobago*		

In countries marked with an asterisk, the rule of the road is Drive on the Left; otherwise Drive on the Right.

Signalling

Travel and communications require efficient systems of signalling. In 1588, when the Spanish Armada threatened to attack Britain, huge bonfires were built on hilltops across the country, and it was arranged that if invasion came, these bonfires would be lit in turn to pass the warning. Later came signal stations on hilltops, relaying messages by means of mirrors reflecting the sun. These were in use by the Royal Navy for sending messages between London and Portsmouth Dockyard from 1795 until 1847. During the last thirty years before the electric telegraph replaced these signal stations, the system in use was the Semaphore Code, using a mast with two arms. Semaphore is now used mainly as a method of flag signalling by scouts, campers and mountaineers.

Semaphore Code

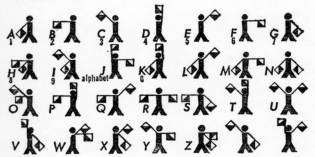

erase number

Before starting a Semaphore message it is customary to hoist the letters 'VOX' or 'I' in International Code flags. Transmission is opened by giving the Alphabetical Sign, then waiting for the signal 'C' in reply as an indication to go ahead. When numbers are to be sent, the Numerical Sign is made; on return to ordinary letters the Alphabetical Sign is given.

International Code

Ships at sea communicate by radio, Morse Code transmitted by signal lamps or the International Code of flag signals. The flag signals are shown on the next page.

An abbreviated code is used for single-flag hoists, to transmit the following standard messages:

A : I am undergoing speed trials.
B : I have explosives on board.
C : Yes.
D : Keep clear, I am in difficulties.
E : I am altering course to starboard.
F : I am disabled.
G : I require a pilot.
H : Pilot is on board.
I : I am altering course to port.
J : I am sending a message by Semaphore.
K : Stop at once.
L : Stop, I wish to communicate with you.
M : A doctor is on board.
N : No.
O : Man overboard.
P : (The Blue Peter) I am about to sail.
Q : Quarantine flag.
R : I have stopped.
S : I am going astern.
T : Do not pass ahead of me.
U : You are in danger.
V : I need help.
W : Send a doctor.
X : Stop, and watch for my signals.
Y : I am carrying mails.
Z : I am calling a shore station.
RY: (flying from the masthead) Crew have mutinied.

Code

A

B

C

D

E

F

G

H

J

K

L

M

J

N

P Blue Peter

Q Quarantine

R

S

T

U

V

W

X

Y

Z

Red

Yellow

Blue

Black

In distress:
Need immediate
assistance

90

The following combinations of two letters on the halyards hoisted to the yardarm signify:

AD: I must abandon my ship.
CG: Alight as near to me as possible.
IX : Seriously damaged in collision.
KA: Vessel is very seriously damaged.
KT: Do you have a line-throwing apparatus?
NC : I am in distress and need immediate assistance.

Morse Code

An American artist, Samuel F. B. Morse (1791—1872), invented the Code that bears his name, to simplify the method of sending messages by telegraph—of which he has equal claim with Britain's Professor Wheatstone to be the inventor. Morse can be sent on a hand key by a skilled operator at up to twenty-five words a minute, but automatic transmitters can exceed this many times, and also 'scramble' the coded message by variations of speed so that only a receiving set equipped with the same system of speed controls can interpret it.

The Code consists of dots and dashes, a dash being equal to three dots. A gap equal to one dot is left between each symbol; twice as much is left between each letter, and a longer break, preferably at least the length of a dash, between words.

The International Morse code is as follows:

A	. —	I	. .
B	— . . .	J	. — — —
C	— . — .	K	— . —
D	— . .	L	. — . .
E	.	M	— —
F	. . — .	N	— .
G	— — .	O	— — —
H	. . . .	P	. — — .

Q	— — . —	1	. — — — —
R	. — .	2	. . — — —
S	. . .	3	. . . — —
T	—	4	. . . . —
U	. . —	5	. . . . .
V	. . . —	6	— . . . .
W	. — —	7	— — . . .
X	— . . —	8	— — — . .
Y	— . — —	9	— — — — .
Z	— — . .	0	— — — — —
Full stop			. — . — . —
Semicolon			— . — . — .
Comma			— — . . — —
Colon			— — — . . .
Interrogation			. . — — . .
Apostrophe			. — — — — .
Hyphen			— . . . . —
Bracket			— . — — . —
Inverted commas			. — . . — .
Underline			. . — — . —
Double dash			— . . . —
Distress signal (S. O. S.)			. . . — — — . . .
Attention signal			— . — . —
Invitation to transmit			— . —
Wait			. — . . .
Break			— . . . —
Understood			. . . — .
Error			. . . .
Received			. — .
Position report			— . — .
End of message			. — . — .
Finish of transmission			. . . — . —

PEOPLE AND LANGUAGE

The Development of the Alphabet We do not know the point in man's development at which he first made sound which could be described as 'language'. The tracing of the history of written language, however, has been possible to a high degree of accuracy, and the diagram on the following page indicates how most of our present-day letters came to be formed.

Column I shows Egyptian hieroglyphics, or picture-writing, facing to the left. Column II is of later Egyptian writing, in which the picture has become unrecognisable, and the direction has changed to the right. Column III shows the progress made by the time of the Phoenicians and Column IV contains the fairly similar alphabet of early Greek civilisation. Columns V, VI and VII show further development by the Greeks; in Columns VIII, IX and X are the stages through which the Romans progressed, leaving as their legacy most of the present-day alphabet of the Western world.

Principal Languages of the World

	Speakers (millions)		Speakers (millions)
Chinese	670	Italian	55
English	275	Javanese	41
Russian	200	Bihari (India)	37
Hindustani	160	Korean	32
Spanish	150	Polish	30
Japanese	91	Telugu (India)	30
German	90	Marathi (India)	27
Arabic	75	Tamil (India)	27
Bengali (India)	75	Malay	25
French	65	Turkish	22
Portuguese	63	Punjabi (India)	21

	EGYPTIAN			GREEK				LATIN		
1				ʼA	A			A	A	aaa
2					B	B	B	B	B	Bb
3					Γ	Γ		⟨	C	c
4				Δ	Δ		δ	D	D	ddd
5					E	E	ε	E	E	ee
6					F		F	F	F	Ff
7				‡	I	Z		‡	Z	z
8				⊟	H	H		⊟	H	hh
9				⊙	⊙	⊖		⊕		
10					I	ι		I	I	ij
11					K	K	KK	K	K	k
12					Λ	λ	λ	L	L	ll
13				M	M	M	MM	M	M	mm
14					N	N			N	nn
15				‡	Ξ		ξ	⊞	+	xx
16					O	O	O	O		
17				Γ	Π	π		P	P	P
18					M		λ			.
19				φ	φ			φ	Q	qq
20					P	P			R	R
21					ξ	C			S	fs
22				T	T	T		T	T	tz

Persian	20	Kanarese (India)	14
Dutch	19	Malayalam (India)	14
Siamese	19	Hungarian	13
Vietnamese	19	Oriya (India)	13
Rajasthani (India)	17	Sudanese	
Rumanian	17	(Indonesia)	13
Burmese	16	Czech	9
Gujarati (India)	16	Greek	9
Serbo-Croat	15	Hausa (Africa)	9

The English Language

Our own language, English, is a mixture of words drawn from the vocabularies of the various invaders of Britain over a period of some two thousand years. That is why in English there are often several different words meaning roughly the same thing, some having Anglo-Saxon origins and others coming from Latin. Our language is also less 'regular' than French, Italian or Spanish, all of which have direct Latin origins.

Words are placed in categories according to how they are used. These categories are known as parts of speech. The English language has eight parts of speech. They are listed below.

Noun : the name of a person, place or thing. Nouns are of four Genders: Masculine, Feminine, Common and Neuter. These Genders can be illustrated by the following words: man, woman, cousin, hat. Nouns are either Singular or Plural, examples of both being: dog and dogs, penny and pence. Classes of nouns are Proper (the name of a particular person, place or thing, e.g. William, France) and Common (the name common to everything in one group, e.g. house, car).

English nouns have three Cases which they take to show their relation to the rest of a sentence. These are Nominative (denoting the person or thing taking action), Objective (the person or thing about which action is taken) and Possessive (that which belongs to a person or thing).

Adjective : a word which describes or qualifies a noun. Adjectives may be divided into three categories : those which express Quality (*bad* company), those expressing Quantity (*ten* boys) and Demonstrative Adjectives (*that* window). There are three degrees of comparison in adjectives—Positive, Comparative and Superlative, examples of which are : good, better, best; young, younger, youngest.

The Articles (Definite : the; Indefinite : a, an) are also adjectives, as are the Numerals (Cardinal : one, two; Ordinal : first, second; Multiplicative : once, twice; Indefinite : many, few).

Pronoun : a word used in place of a noun. Pronouns, like nouns, have Gender, Number and Case. Pronouns may be Personal (I, she, you), Relative (that, who), Demonstrative (this, those), Indefinite (some, one), Interrogative (who? which?), Distributive (either, each) and Reflexive (yourself, themselves).

Verb : a word which states the action of a noun. Verbs are either Transitive or Intransitive. Transitive verbs describe an action which affects an object, e.g. 'I start the car'. Intransitive verbs do not affect an object, e.g. 'The car starts.' 'I start the car' is an example of a verb in Active Voice; in Passive Voice it would be 'The car was started by me.'

Verbs have three Finite Moods : Indicative (I speak); Imperative (Speak!); Subjunctive (I may speak). There is also the Infinitive Mood (to speak).

There are two Participles, used with such verbs as *to be* and *to have :* the Present Participle (speaking) and the Past Participle (spoken). There is also a verbal noun, the Gerund (the *speaking* of English).

The Tense of a verb shows the time of its action (Past, Present, Future). The degrees of completeness of the action are : Simple (I speak, I spoke, I shall speak); Continuous

96

(I am speaking; I was speaking, I shall be speaking); Perfect (I have spoken, I had spoken, I shall have spoken); Perfect Continuous (I have been speaking, I had been speaking, I shall have been speaking).

Adverb : a word which modifies or qualifies a verb, an adjective or another adverb. Adverbs can be divided into the following categories: Time (often, now); Place (here, outside); Quality (well, beautifully); Quantity (enough, almost); Number (once); Cause (therefore, why); Mood (perhaps).

Preposition : a word which shows the relation between words in a sentence. Examples of prepositions are: to, on, by, of, from, for, through, about, after, except, towards.

Conjunction : a word which links words, phrases, clauses or sentences. Examples of conjunctions are: and, but, for, because, also, unless, though, therefore.

Interjection : a word standing alone in a sentence, expressing strong emotion. Examples are: Indeed! Goodness! Bother! Oh! Alas!

Foreign Words and Phrases

There are many foreign expressions used in English, a number of which are quite convenient in that there is no exact equivalent in our language. Here are some in common use (Abbreviations—F: French; G: German; Gk: Greek; I: Italian; L: Latin; P: Portuguese; S: Spanish).

ad hoc (L). For this special object.
ad infinitum (L). For ever; to infinity.
ad interim (L). Meanwhile.
ad libitum (ad lib.) (L). To any extent; at pleasure.
ad nauseam (L). To the point of disgust.
adsum (L). I am here.
ad valorem (L). According to value.
affaire d'honneur (F). Affair of honour; duel.
a fortiori (L). With stronger reason.
à la bonne heure (F). Well done; that's good.

à la carte (F). From the full menu.
à la mode (F). In the fashion.
alter ego (L). Other self.
amour-propre (F). Self-esteem.
a posteriori (L). From the effect to the cause.
a priori (L). From the cause to the effect.
à propos (F). To the point.
arrière-pensée (F). Mental reservation.
au contraire (F). On the contrary.
au courant (F). Fully acquainted (with).
auf Wiedersehen (G). Till we meet again.
au naturel (F). In a natural state.
au pair (F). On an exchange basis.
au revoir (F). Till we meet again.
auto da fé (P). Act of faith.
à votre santé (F). Your good health!

bête noire (F). Pet hate.
billet doux (F). Love letter.
bona fide (L). In good faith; genuine.
bon marché (F). A bargain; cheap.
bon vivant (F). Gourmet; one who enjoys life.
bon voyage (F). Have a good journey.

canaille (F). Common mob (term of contempt).
carpe diem (L). Enjoy today.
carte blanche (F). Full powers.
casus belli (L). Cause of war.
caveat emport (L). Let the buyer beware.
chacun à son goût (F). Everyone to his own taste.
chef-d'oeuvre (F). Masterpiece.
cherchez la femme (F). Look for the woman (in the case).
ci-devant (F). Former.
comme il faut (F). In good taste.
compos mentis (L). In full possession of sanity.

corps de ballet (F). The team of dancers in a ballet.
corps diplomatique (F). The group of diplomats in a capital city.
cui bono? (L). Who will get any benefit?
cum grano salis (L). With a grain of salt.

d'accord (F). Agreed.
de facto (L). In fact.
de jure (L). By right (in law).
de luxe (F). Of especially high quality.
de rigueur (F). Necessary.
dernier cri (F). The latest fashion.
de trop (F). Superfluous; not wanted.
deus ex machina (L). Providential interposition; nick-of-time solution by a superhuman agency.
Dieu et mon droit (F). God and my right (motto of the British Crown).
double entente (F). Double meaning (sometimes *double entendre*).

embarras de richesse (F). Difficulty caused by having too much.
en deshabillé (F). Dressed in clothes suitable only for lounging.
en famille (F). In the family; informal.
en fête (F). Celebrating.
en passant (F). In passing; by the way.
en rapport (F). In sympathy; in harmony.
entre nous (F). Between ourselves.
esprit de corps (F). Group spirit.
ex cathedra (L). From the chair of office, with authority.
ex libris (L). From the books (of).

fait accompli (F). An accomplished fact.
faux pas (F). False step; mistake.
femme de chambre (F). Chambermaid.

fête champêtre (F). Gala occasion in the open air.
fiat lux (L). Let there be light.
fin de siècle (F). Decadent.

gitano (S). Gipsy.
gourmet (F). Lover of good food.

Hausfrau (G). Housewife.
hic jacet (L). Here lies.
hoi polloi (Gk). The people.
honi soit qui mal y pense (F). Shamed be he who thinks evil of it.
hors de combat (F). No longer able to fight.

ibidem (ibid.) (L). In the same place.
ich dien (G). I serve.
idée fixe (F). Obsession.
in extremis (L). At the point of death.
infra dignitatem (infra dig.) (L). Beneath one's dignity.
in loco parentis (L). In the place of a parent.
in memoriam (L). In memory (of).
in perpetuum (L). For ever.
in re (L). In the matter of.
in situ (L). In its original position.
inter alia (L). Among other things.
in toto (L). Completely.
ipso facto (L). (Obvious) from the facts.
ipso jure (L). By the law itself.

je ne sais quoi (F). I know not what.
jeu d'esprit (F). Witticism.

laissez faire (F). Leave matters alone: a policy of non-interference.
lares et penates (L). Household gods.
lèse-majesté (F). High treason or arrogant conduct of inferiors.

locum tenens (L). A substitute or deputy.

magnum opus (L). A great work; an author's principal book

maitre d'hôtel (F). Hotel-keeper; head waiter.

mal de mer (F). Sea-sickness.

mañana (S). Tomorrow (will do as well as today).

mariage de convenance (F). A marriage arranged for money or other material considerations.

mea culpa (L). It is my fault.

modus operandi (L). Method of working.

multum in parvo (L). Much in little.

mutatis mutandis (L). The necessary changes having been made.

non plus ultra (L). Nothing further; the summit of achievement.

nil desperandum (L). Despair of nothing.

noblesse oblige (F). Noble birth imposes obligations.

nom de guerre (F). Assumed name.

nom de plume (F). Assumed name of an author.

non compos mentis (L). Of unsound mind.

non sequitur (L). It does not follow.

nota bene (N. B.) (L). Note well.

nouveau riche (F). Newly rich.

opus (L). Work (of art, music or literature).

outré (F). Eccentric; outside the bounds of propriety.

pace (L). By leave of.

par excellence (F). Pre-eminently.

par exemple (F). For example.

passim (L). Everywhere.

pax vobiscum (L). Peace be with you.

per annum (L). By the year.

per capita (L). By the head.

per centum (per cent) (L). By the hundred.
per diem (L). By the day.
per mensem (L). By the month.
persona grata (L). An acceptable person.
persona non grata (L). An unacceptable person.
pièce de résistance (F). Chief dish of meal; main item.
pied-à-terre (F). Lodging for occasional visits.
poste restante (F). To await collection (from a post office).
prima ballerina (I). Principal female dancer in a ballet.
prima donna (I). Principal female singer in an opera.
prima facie (L). At first sight.
pro forma (L). As a matter of form.
pro rata (L). In proportion.
prosit (G). Good health!
pro tempore (L). For the time being.

quid pro quo (L). Something offered for another of the same value.
quien sabe? (S). Who knows?
quo vadis (L). Whither thou goest?

raison d'être (F). Reason for existence.
rara avis (L). A rare bird; unusual person or thing.
reduction ad absurdum (L). A reducing to the absurd.
rendez-vous (F). Meeting-place.
requiescat in pace (L). Rest in peace.
résumé (F). Summary.

sans souçi (F). Without care.
sauve qui peut (F). Save himself who can.
savoir-faire (F). Tact.
semper fidelis (L). Always faithful.
sine die (L). Indefinitely.
sine qua non (L). An indispensable condition.
sobriquet (F). Nickname.
soi-disant (F). Self-styled.

sotto voce (I). In a whisper or undertone.
status quo (L). The existing state of affairs.
stet (L). Let it stand (ignore correction marks).
sub judice (L). Before a judge (and not yet decided).
sub rosa (L). Under the rose; secretly.
sui generis (L). Of its own kind; unique.

table d'hôte (F). A set meal at a fixed price.
tempus fugit (L). Time flies.
terra firma (L). Solid earth.
tête-à-tête (F). Private talk between two people.
tour de force (F). Feat of skill or strength.
tout de suite (F). Immediately.
tout ensemble (F). Taken all together.

ubique (L). Everywhere.
ultima Thule (L). The utmost boundary.

vade mecum (L). A constant companion; a manual of reference.
versus (L). Against.
vice versa (L). Conversely.
vis-à-vis (F). Opposite; face to face.

wagon-lit (F). Railway sleeping-car.
Weltschmerz (G). World weariness.

Zeitgeist (G). Spirit of the times.

PEOPLE AND SCIENCE

Nowadays a higher proportion of people than ever before live in well-built houses, have enough to eat, are well clothed and have at birth an expectation of life of some sixty to seventy years. Two centuries ago this expectation of life was not much more than half the present figure, for lack of medical knowledge together with poor living conditions resulted in much ill health and in epidemics which wiped out huge sections of the population at a single stroke.

Science has changed all this—through researches in medicine and agriculture, by finding ways to make the things we need more rapidly and more cheaply and by discovering new substances out of which we can construct the complicated machinery of the modern world.

Here are some of the techniques developed by science in the past two centuries.

Brick-making by Machine

Most countries have clay suitable for brick-making. This is dug out of the ground by mechanical shovels, then fed into a system of huge rollers which crush it into a fine, powdery substance. Moisture is added, and a band of clay is forced through a hole and then cut into individual bricks by wires. The wet bricks are slowly dried, then put in a kiln and baked at a high temperature.

Cement Manufacture

Modern building technique is very largely dependent on cement. Clay, chalk and limestone are crushed, then fed into a machine which mixes them with water into a thick cream.

This cream, known as 'slurry', is conveyed to a high-temperature kiln which reduces it to clinker. The clinker passes between a series of rollers which grind it up, and the pale grey powder which results is cement. For building purposes this is mixed in a revolving drum with sand and water, using proportions of from three to five shovels of sand to each shovel of cement. For concrete, up to six shovels of 'aggregate' (a mixture of sand and small stones) is used with each shovel of cement.

Electric Power

This is produced by using water power, some form of fuel, or atomic energy (see section on **Nuclear Power**). The pressure of water from a dam, or, alternatively, steam created by burning fuel, turns a dynamo. The rotation of this spins a rotor. The rotor is an electro-magnet, which, surrounded by a coil of wire, sets up an electric current in the wire.

Gas Production

Still the principal source of heat for household cooking, gas is made by baking coal in a container or retort. The gas given off is stored in gasometers until required. By-products of the process include petrol, acids, drugs, perfumes, dyes, tar and coke. Natural gas from the North Sea is being used in Britain for commercial and domestic purposes.

Glass-making

The method of glass manufacture has changed little over the centuries, but the speed and mechanisation have been greatly increased. Specially selected sand is mixed with limestone and soda ash and melted until liquid. It is then rolled out to make plate glass, moulded to make the cheaper kind of jars, tumblers and bottles, or blown into shape for high-quality articles. Glass-blowing is still done by hand; the blower dips a long tube into the molten glass, then blows through the tube as if inflating a balloon.

Paper Manufacture

The tremendous output of books and newspapers today means that many thousands of tons of paper have to be made every year. What was once a laborious process carried out by hand is now a highly mechanised industry. Paper is made of esparto grass, rag, wood-pulp or various mixtures of these materials. These are reduced to a fibrous pulp, boiled, and bleached. The pulp then travels along a moving belt over a suction chamber which removes excess moisture. The sheet which is formed through this process goes between rollers and drying cylinders until it emerges as a roll of white paper.

Printing

Modern printing has come a long way since 1474 when William Caxton printed the first book in the English language. Today millions of newspapers, magazines and books are produced on fast, modern printing machines. Three main methods of printing are used. The first, probably the oldest, is called Letterpress. This involves raised metal letters, or characters. Ink is applied and the paper pressed on to them. This book is printed by Letterpress.

The second method, also very old in origin, has been developed extensively only in the last twenty years. This is called Offset Lithography and employs a photographically prepared plate which is inked. Because of the way it is made, only the areas which are required to print accept the ink. This then prints on to a rubber covered cylinder which in turn prints, or offsets, on to the paper.

The third method, Gravure, is used mainly for magazine printing. Small holes of varying depth are etched into a plate.

This is first inked. A special blade called a 'doctor blade' scrapes away the unwanted surface ink leaving only that which is trapped in the holes. Paper is then pressed against the plate and the ink is drawn out on to it.

The two types of printing machines used are sheet-fed and rotary. Sheet-fed is used mainly for books, and prints the sheets of paper one at a time. Rotary is mainly used for newspapers, printing a continuous reel of paper, which is cut and folded afterwards.

Spinning

Two hundred years of progress in spinning have speeded up the process rather than changed the method. The original spinning-wheel produced one thread at a time. The wool, after washing, carding to remove lumps and combing to place the hairs in one direction, was twisted and rolled into yarn. The modern spinning machine does this to hundreds of threads at the same time.

Steel Manufacture

To make steel from cast iron it is necessary to remove certain substances which exist in it as impurities, the chief of which is carbon. The method of removal is generally by means of an open-hearth furnace, in which pigs, or bars, of cast iron, are raised to a great heat by burning gas and air fed into the hearth at high pressure. The molten steel is poured into moulds, and the ingots thus made pass between rollers which press them into girders.

Water Supply and Drainage

Water as it comes from most rivers is not pure enough to drink. Also, we cannot depend on a river for supplies at all times of the year. The solutions to these two problems are purification and the use of reservoirs. River water, pumped into a reservoir, is taken out as required and placed in tanks containing purifying chemicals. From these, it flows to open tanks in which there are layers of gravel that filter away impurities. The final stage involves the addition of still more chemicals, and the water is then kept in covered tanks and reservoirs until pumped through the mains to individual houses.

Hot water is produced in the modern house by one of three methods: gas, electricity or solid fuel. In the first method, water is led over powerful burners, usually by means of a spiral tube, so that while the outlet tap is running the water is receiving heat from the burners. Water is warmed electrically by means of an immersion heater, which is an electric heating element, protected by a tube, placed inside a water tank. Heating water by a solid fuel stove requires an enclosed fire containing a water-jacket or an open fire with a back-boiler device. From the cold-water tank in the loft water runs down to the hot-water tank (often in a cupboard), and from there down a pipe to the bottom of the water-jacket. As the fire heats the water it rises up a second pipe to the hot-water tank. It is replaced automatically by colder water coming down the first pipe, and the circulation provides a constant supply of hot water in the tank from which yet another pipe leads out, at the top, to supply the hot taps in the kitchen and bathroom.

Our modern drainage system is just as important as our water supply. In the past, refuse was thrown into open drains in the streets. Insects and germs breeding in these drains spread disease. Modern sewers all run below ground. The 'U' tube under the sink, bath and W.C., in which water always remains, prevents gases and unpleasant smells from coming up from the sewers into which the waste pipes lead. When the sewage reaches the sewage farm it is mechanically sieved to remove grit which is later used for concrete and road-works. Then the solids are separated from the liquids in settling tanks. The liquids are agitated by a jet of compressed air, which makes the bacteria multiply rapidly and breaks down any remaining solids into small particles. The final products are a harmless liquid which can be released into a river or the sea, and mud which, when fermented, gives off a gas that supplies the main source of power of the sewage farm.

The following inventions have also done much to change the world in recent times.

Camera

Light entering a darkened box through a small hole will project an image inside the box of the scene outside—but in reverse and upside-down. In practice a lens with a shutter is used instead of a small hole, in order to admit more light. A sensitised plate or film at the back of the camera receives the impression. The film or plate is then removed in a dark room, where it is immersed in chemical solutions. This process produces a negative, with its black objects white and *vice versa*. A positive, or print, is made by placing the negative on sensitised paper and exposing it to the light, whereupon the white portions of the negative admit light. The sensitised paper is then treated with chemicals, and the original image appears.

Diesel Engine

This is a very high compression internal combustion engine. Air is drawn into a cylinder and compressed to about five hundred pounds per square inch. This raises its temperature to a point where, when fuel oil is pumped in, it immediately ignites and creates the explosion necessary to force the piston down.

Internal Combustion Engine

This is the name for the petrol engine used in cars, motorcycles and light lorries. A carburettor converts petrol into a fine vapour, and also draws in air which mixes with it. The mixture travels through a valve system into the top of a cylinder and is there exploded under pressure by means of an electric sparking plug. The explosion forces down the piston, from which a connecting rod runs to a crank-shaft. On its return stroke the piston pushes out the burned gases through the valve system; its next journey down draws in a fresh supply of fuel, and its upward journey compresses the fuel in readiness for the next explosion.

Jet Engine

Turbojet. Modern aircraft are frequently fitted with turbojet engines, as they develop far greater power than piston engines. They run on paraffin, which is burned with compressed air to produce expanding gases which drive the blades of a turbine. On the same axle another turbine forces air into the firing chamber. The turbojet propels by forcing out a jet of hot air at its rear. The turboprop, a later development, uses its turbine to turn an air-screw.

Ramjet. This is an engine intended to 'take over' an aircraft once it has reached a speed of roughly two hundred miles an hour. Air is forced in at the nose of the engine, fuel is burned in it, and the resultant high pressure produces a propellent exhaust. The ramjet becomes more efficient as it gains speed, for speed adds to the intake of air and therefore to the potential thrust.

Hovercraft

Though neither an aircraft nor a boat, this British invention is an entirely new form of transport. Basically, it is a round boat with a flat bottom. In the centre of the vehicle is an engine which drives air down through the bottom of the boat. For this air to escape, it must raise the hull. Hence the hovering. To travel forward, another engine (either jet or more normally rotor bladed) is used. The Hovercraft is limited in its uses as it can travel across only fairly smooth land or water. However, its first commercial test came when Hovercrafts were ordered by a fruit company to transport bananas across previously inaccessible swampland, and as the engines are increased in efficiency, they will allow the Hovercraft to travel higher above the ground and therefore clear larger waves or land obstacles. They are now in use for passengers and cars between Britain and France, and also between the mainland and the Isle of Wight.

Plastics

There are two types—thermosetting and thermoplastic. The latter can be reshaped by the application of heat, but the former are subjected to heat during manufacture, and once moulded cannot be altered in shape. Thermoplastics include acrylic, vinyl and polystyrene—all in common use for household purposes and in toy-making. Many plastics are formed by treating coal derivatives such as phenol.

Steam Locomotion

Basically, the modern steam locomotive uses the same system as George Stephenson's original *Rocket*. Coal or oil is burned to produce fierce heat and create super-heated steam. This passes in controlled quantities to the cylinders, in turn pushing the pistons back and forth by being admitted to each cylinder first at one end and then at the other. This backwards and forwards movement is converted into a circular movement by connecting rods joined off-centre to the main driving wheels of the locomotive, and is passed from one main wheel to the next by coupling rods.

Submarine

The main sea-weapon in any future war would probably be the submarine, because of its proved worth in disrupting supply lines by sinking merchant ships and also because it is an ideal launching platform for short-range guided missiles. The principle of the submarine is that of double-shell construction. The crew's quarters and the engine rooms are in an airtight shell, and between this and the outer shell are diving tanks. To submerge the submarine, these tanks are flooded by opening a series of valves. To return to the surface, powerful pumps are used to clear the tanks.

Propulsion is by Diesel engine, battery-driven electric motors and, recently, nuclear power.

Great Inventions and Discoveries

Discovery or Invention	Person Responsible	Country	Year
Aeroplane	Wilbur and Orville Wright	United States	1903
Airship	Henri Giffard	France	1852
Atomic Structure	Lord Rutherford	Britain	1910–1
Balloon	Joseph and Jacques Montgolfier	France	1783
Barometer	Evangelista Toricelli	Italy	1643
Bicycle	Kirkpatrick MacMillan	Britain	1839
Clock, Pendulum	Christiaan Huygens	Netherlands	1656
Diesel Engine	Rudolf Diesel	Germany	1897
Dynamite	Alfred Nobel	Sweden	1867
Dynamo	Michael Faraday	Britain	1831
Electric Arc Lamp	Sir Humphry Davy	Britain	1809

Electric Battery	Alessandro Volta	Italy	1800
Food Preservation (in tins)	Francois Appert	France	1810
Gas Lighting	William Murdock	Britain	1792
Gramophone	Thomas A. Edison	United States	1877
Helicopter	Louis G. Bréguet	France	1909
Locomotive, Steam	Richard Trevithick	Britain	1801
Match, Friction	John Walker	Britain	1827
Match, Safety	J. E. Lundstrom	Sweden	1855
Microscope, Compound	Zacharias Janssen	Netherlands	1590
Motion-picture Camera	William Friese-Greene	Britain	1888
Motor-car	Gottlieb Daimler	Germany	1887
Nylon	E. I. du Pont de Nemours & Co.	United States	1938
Parachute	J. P. Blanchard	France	1785
Penicillin	Sir Alexander Fleming	Britain	1929
Photography	J. Nicéphore Niepce	France	1822
Pianoforte	Bartolommeo Cristofori	Italy	1709
Postage Stamp	Sir Rowland Hill	Britain	1840
Power Loom	Edmund Cartwright	Britain	1786
Printing, Movable Type	Johann Gutenberg	Germany	c. 1440
Radium	Pierre and Marie Curie	France	1898
Safety Lamp, Miner's	Sir Humphry Davy	Britain	1816
Sewing Machine	Walter Hunt	United States	1832
Sextant	John Hadley	Britain	1731

Smallpox Vaccination	Edward Jenner	Britain	1796
Steam Engine	James Watt	Britain	1769
Steam Turbine	Sir Charles A. Parsons	Britain	1884
Tank	Sir Ernest Swinton	Britain	1914
Telegraph. Elektro-magnetic	Samuel F. B. Morse	United States	1838
Telephone	Alexander Graham Bell	United States	1876
Thermometer, Mercury-in-glass	Gabriel Daniel Fahrenheit	Germany	1714
Torpedo (Modern)	Robert Whitehead	Britain	1868
Tungsten-fila-ment Lamp	Irving Langmuir	United States	1913
Typewriter	Christopher Sholes	United States	1868
Wireless	Guglielmo Marconi	Italy	1895
X-rays	Wilhelm Roentgen	Germany	1895

Journeys into Space

We live in the age of man's fastest scientific progress. His curiosity takes him to the Poles, to the deepest parts of the ocean and many miles high into the sky.

What is the sum total so far in the exploration of space—and what may lie ahead within your own lifetime?

The first space 'probes' were the two Russian satellites, *Sputnik I*, and *Sputnik II*, in 1957, which were propelled by multiple-stage rockets to a distance of several hundred miles above the earth's surface, and then directed into orbit so that they circled the earth on a definite course at a speed of about 18,000 miles per hour.

The Americans launched their first satellites in the early part of 1958, and then, in October, fired a multiple-stage rocket designed to explore the Moon. It was equipped with television gear and it was hoped that it would send back a picture of the far side of the Moon—the side which had never been seen by man.

This was a failure; at some 80,000 feet the flight ended and the object returned to the earth's atmosphere.

In September 1959, the Russian rocket *Lunik II* reached the Moon and photographed its far side.

In August 1960, another Russian rocket was put into orbit containing two dogs. This satellite reached its target back on Earth with the dogs unharmed. In the spring of 1961, the Americans made a similarly successful flight with a chimpanzee.

Then on 12 April of that year came the first man in space, when the Russians sent up Major Yuri Gagarin who made one orbit of the world before landing. This was improved on when fellow-Russian Major Gherman Titov made 17 orbits on August 6, 1961.

Much of America's space prestige was restored when they sent up their first astronaut on February 20, 1962, Colonel John Glenn making three orbits in his *Friendship 7*. This was followed by another three-orbit flight by Major Scott Carpenter in his space capsule *Aurora 7*. Since then, further flights in space have been carried out successfully, unmanned rockets have been fired to the Moon, and information satellites have been launched. In 1965, *Mariner IV* (U.S.A.) sent back to Earth close-up pictures of the surface of Mars, and Major Virgil Grissom (first man to fly twice in space) and Lt. Cdr. John Young completed a two-man American space mission, manoeuvring their craft's height and direction in orbit for the first time. On 15th December, 1965, America's *Gemini VI* and *VII* effected the first-ever human meeting in space. Meanwhile, also in 1965, Col. Belyaev piloted a two-man Russian spaceship while his companion,

Lt. Col. Leonov, became the first man to walk out into space, floating at the end of a 15 ft. lifeline for 20 minutes.

In 1967, both American and Russian space probes landed on the Moon and sent information about its surface back to the Earth.

The American space programme reached its climax in July 1969 when the huge Saturn V rocket blasted off from Cape Kennedy carrying Apollo XI and the three-man crew, Neil Armstrong, Edwin Aldrin and Michael Collins. In the early hours of 21 July Neil Armstrong became the first human being to set foot on the Moon. He was followed by Aldrin, while Collins piloted the command module orbiting above.

America's 1971 *Apollo 15* mission to the Moon proved an enormous success. That same year the Russians also made a major breakthrough when *Soyuz 11* docked with the *Salyut* space station. This proved the feasiblity of space stations orbiting for long periods, manned by a succession of astronauts and scientists. The Americans then launched Skylab in 1972, an experimetal venture in their plans for space stations.

Nuclear Power and its Peaceful Uses

Nuclear power—born of the research which made the first atomic bomb—is now being harnessed to peaceful uses and will change man's whole pattern of living. But what is nuclear power, and how do we make it work for us?

It was a New Zealand scientist working in Britain, Lord Rutherford, who did much of the pioneer research which revealed the enormous power dormant in the nucleus of the atom—power enough to provide the world with unlimited resources, power which could heat every house and factory in the world, pump water to every desert on the globe and turn every machine-wheel man can create. His problem was how to release that power and how to do so safely.

116

What is an atom? The nuclear theory of the atom, which was put forward by Rutherford and his colleague Sir Joseph Thomson, was published as long ago as 1911. The atom consists of a minutely small but very heavy nucleus containing a positive electric charge; round this circulate much lighter electrons having a total negative electric charge which exactly equals the positive charge of the nucleus. In 1932 Sir James Chadwick discovered that the nucleus consists of protons, which are electrically positive, and neutrons, which are neutral.

How does power come into all this? All matter is made up of atoms of elements, and certain elements have atoms which are known as 'unstable'—meaning that the nucleus can be upset, giving off a tremendous amount of power. Once started, this process can be continued in what is known as a controlled chain reaction, providing a steady supply of power in the form of heat.

An atomic pile, or power unit, is made up of carbon blocks in which are placed rods of the unstable element uranium. Control of the heat is maintained by means of other rods, of boron or cadmium, either of which has the effect of slowing down nuclear reaction. These rods can be raised or lowered in the pile to regulate its output as the temperature drops or increases.

Putting the heat to practical use is done by forcing carbon dioxide through the pile by means of pumps. The gas emerges at high temperature and operates steam turbine generators which supply electricity to the National Grid.

The world's first economically practical atomic generator was put into use in Britain at Calder Hall, in 1956, and since then generators of various patterns, but operating on the same basic principles, have been working in the United States and Russia. Countries with less money and smaller industrial resources have formed groups such as the European Organisation for Nuclear Research, to provide themselves with the equipment to carry out their own experiments

117

towards more advanced systems of developing atomic power. But the story of nuclear power does not end with the setting up of hundreds of generators throughout the world to make us independent of coal and oil. Generators which depend on uranium to provide the active heart of the pile are expensive, as uranium is a rare metal. The next step is cheap nuclear power, and this seems likely to come from a hydrogen reactor. As the atomic reactor depends on the principle of the atomic bomb—fission—the hydrogen reactor depends on that of the hydrogen bomb, which is fusion. It is actually the fusion of light elements into heavier ones which produces the power in this case. The principle is the one which provides the sun's energy. Scientists hope to produce hydrogen reactors costing little to run and yielding electric power direct, without turbines and generators.

If they succeed, man will truly have achieved a limitless source of useful power.

Anatomy

Like big buildings the body is constructed round a framework of girders. To this frame or skeleton all the muscles and important organs are attached.

The backbone (spine) is made up of ring-like bones, and down the middle runs the spinal cord. At the top of the spine is the head, which is like a bone box protecting the brain.

Attached to the spine is a cage of bones, the ribs, which protect the heart, lungs and liver. These ribs are joined at the front to the breast-bone.

To this breast-bone are joined the two collar-bones, and to these the two shoulder-blades and to these the arms.

At the lower end of the spine is the pelvis, to which are attached the legs.

The upper arms and thighs have one bone each; the forearms and lower legs, two bones each. The wrists and ankles contain groups of small square bones. Longer ones are in the

118

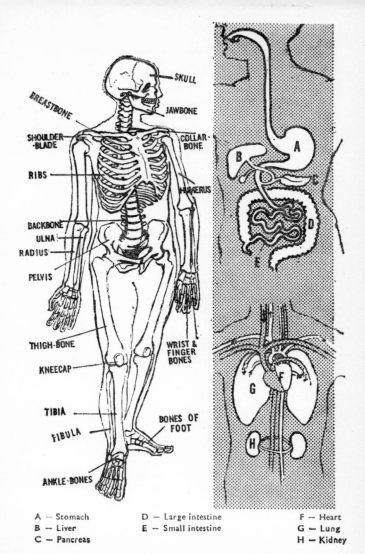

SKULL

BREASTBONE

JAWBONE

SHOULDER-BLADE

COLLAR-BONE

RIBS

HUMERUS

BACKBONE

ULNA

RADIUS

PELVIS

THIGH-BONE

WRIST & FINGER BONES

KNEECAP

TIBIA

BONES OF FOOT

FIBULA

ANKLE-BONES

A — Stomach   D — Large intestine   F — Heart
B — Liver   E — Small intestine   G — Lung
C — Pancreas   H — Kidney

palms and soles of the feet, and not quite such long ones in the fingers and toes.

There are seven major organs which carry out the various functions of the body.

The brain directs the body's working by receiving messages through the nervous system and by sending messages to other parts of the body along the spinal cord and nerves.

The heart pumps the blood through the body by way of the arteries, and receives it back through the veins.

The lungs take air into the body by means of the upper respiratory tract. They also expel carbon dioxide, a waste product taken from the blood.

The stomach takes in food, begins the digestive process and sends the food through the intestines to complete digestion.

The liver and the pancreas discharge juices into the small intestine which aid in the digestion of food. The liver also stores vitamins, and aids in purifying the blood, while the pancreas regulates the amount of sugar in the blood.

The kidneys remove waste materials from the blood. These waste materials are carried to the bladder, where they are kept until evacuated from the body.

Weights and Measures

Weights. Imperial System (used in Britain and certain Commonwealth lands).

Avoirdupois Weight

27.34	grains	=	1 dram
16	drams	=	1 ounce
16	ounces	=	1 pound
14	pounds	=	1 stone
28	pounds	=	1 quarter
4	quarters	=	1 hundredweight
20	hundredweights	=	1 ton

120

Troy Weight (used by jewellers)

3.17	grains	=	1 carat
24	grains	=	1 pennyweight
20	pennyweights	=	1 ounce
12	ounces	=	1 pound
100	pounds	=	1 hundredweight

Apothecaries' Weight

20 grains	=	1 scruple
3 scruples	=	1 drachm
8 drachms	=	1 ounce
12 ounces	=	1 pound

Weights. Metric System

10 milligrams	=	1 centigram
10 centigrams	=	1 decigram
10 decigrams	=	1 gram
10 grams	=	1 decagram
10 decagrams	=	1 hectogram
10 hectograms	=	1 kilogram
10 kilograms	=	1 myriagram
10 myriagrams	=	1 quintal
10 quintals	=	1 metric ton

Weight Conversions

1 grain	=	0.0648 grams
1 dram	=	1.772 grams
1 ounce	=	2.835 decagrams
	=	(28.35 grams)

121

1 pound	=	0.454	kilograms
1 stone	=	6.35	kilograms
1 quarter	=	12.7	kilograms
1 hundedweight	=	50.8	kilograms
1 ton	=	1.016	metric tons
1 milligram	=	0.015	grains
1 centigram	=	0.154	grains
1 decigram	=	1.543	grains
1 gram	=	15.432	grains
1 decagram	=	5.644	drams
1 hectogram	=	3.527	ounces
1 kilogram	=	2.205	pounds
1 myriagram	=	22	pounds
1 quintal	=	1.968	hundredweights
1 metric ton	=	0.9842	tons

Measures. Imperial System

Linear Measure

12	inches	=	1 foot
3	feet	=	1 yard
5½	yards	=	1 rod, pole or perch
22	yards	=	1 chain
10	chains	=	1 furlong
8	furlongs	=	1 mile
			(1,760 yards; 5,280 feet)
3	miles	=	1 league

Square Measure

144	square inches	=	1 square foot
9	square feet	=	1 square yard
30¼	square yards	=	1 square rod, pole or perch

40	square rods	=	1 rood
4	roods (4,840 square yards)	=	1 acre
640	acres	=	1 square mile

Capacity Measure

4	gills	=	1 pint
2	pints	=	1 quart
4	quarts	=	1 gallon (0.833 Imperial gallons = 1 U.S. gallon)
2	gallons	=	1 peck
4	pecks	=	1 bushel
8	bushels	=	1 quarter
4½	quarters	=	1 chaldron

Cubic Measure

1,728	cubic inches	=	1 cubic foot
27	cubic feet	=	1 cubic yard

Measures. Metric System

Linear Measure

10	millimetres	=	1 centimetre
10	centimetres	=	1 decimetre
10	decimetres	=	1 metre
10	metres	=	1 decametre
10	decametres	=	1 hectometre
10	hectometres	=	1 kilometre
10	kilometres	=	1 myriametre

Square Measure

100 square millimetres	=	1 square centimetre
100 square centimetres	=	1 square decimetre
100 square metres	=	1 are
100 ares	=	1 hectare
100 hectares	=	1 square kilometre

Capacity Measure

10 millilitres	=	1 centilitre
10 centilitres	=	1 decilitre
10 decilitres	=	1 litre
10 litres	=	1 decalitre
10 decalitres	=	1 hectolitre
10 hectolitres	=	1 kilolitre

Cubic Measure

1,000 cubic millimetres	=	1 cubic centimetre
1,000 cubic centimetres	=	1 cubic decimetre
1,000 cubic decimetres	=	1 cubic metre

Measure Conversions

Linear Measure

1 inch	=	2.54	centimetres
1 foot	=	30.48	centimetres
1 yard	=	0.9144	metres
1 rod	=	5.029	metres
1 chain	=	20.116	metres
1 furlong	=	201.16	metres
1 mile	=	1.6093	kilometres

1 millimetre	=	0.03937	inches
1 centimetre	=	0.3937	inches
1 decimetre	=	3.937	inches
1 metre	=	39.37	inches
		(1.0936	yards)
1 decametre	=	10.936	yards
1 hectometre	=	109.36	yards
1 kilometre	=	0.62137	miles

Square Measure

1 square inch	=	6.4514	square centimetres
1 square foot	=	9.29	square decimetres
1 square yard	=	0.836	square metres
1 square rod	=	25.293	square metres
1 rood	=	10.117	ares
1 acre	=	0.405	hectares
1 square mile	=	259	hectares
1 square centimetre	=	0.155	square inches
1 square metre	=	10.764	square feet
		(1,196	square yards)
1 are	=	119.6	square yards
1 hectare	=	2.47	acres

Cubic Measure

1 cubic inch	=	16.387	cubic centimetres
1 cubic foot	=	0.0283	cubic metres
1 cubic yard	=	0.7646	cubic metres
1 cubic centimetre	=	0.061	cubic inches
1 cubic decimetre	=	61.024	cubic inches
1 cubic metre	=	35.315	cubic feet
		(1.308	cubic yards)

125

Capacity Measure

1 gill	=	1.42	decilitres
1 pint	=	0.568	litres
1 quart	=	1.136	litres
1 gallon	=	4.546	litres
1 bushel	=	36.37	gallons
		(3.637	decalitres)
1 quarter	=	2.91	hectolitres
1 centilitre	=	0.07	gills
1 decilitre	=	0.176	pints
1 litre	=	1.7598	pints
1 decalitre	=	2.2	gallons
1 hectolitre	=	2.75	bushels
		(21.99	gallons)

Nautical Measures

6 feet	=	1 fathom
100 fathoms	=	1 cable
10 cables (6,080 feet)	=	1 nautical mile
1 knot	=	1 nautical mile *per hour*

Other Measures

1 tablespoon	=	$\frac{1}{2}$ fluid ounce
1 dessertspoon	=	$\frac{1}{4}$ fluid ounce
1 teaspoon	=	$\frac{1}{8}$ fluid ounce

Miscellaneous

1 gallon of water weighs 10 pounds.

1 horsepower is the power required to raise 550 pounds by 1 foot in 1 second.

1 kilowatt is the power required to raise 737.6 pounds by 1 foot in 1 second.

Measure and Sizes for Paper and Books

Imperial Paper Sizes

Foolscap	$13\frac{1}{2} \times 17$ ins.
Large Post	$16\frac{1}{2} \times 21$ ins.
Demy	$17\frac{1}{2} \times 22\frac{1}{2}$ ins.
Medium	18×23 ins.
Crown	15×20 ins.
Royal	20×25 ins.

Metric Paper Sizes

A0	841×1189 mm
A1	594×841 mm
A2	420×594 mm
A3	297×420 mm
A4	210×297 mm
RA0	860×1220 mm
RA1	610×860 mm
RA2	430×610 mm
SRA0	900×1280 mm
SRA1	640×900 mm
SRA2	450×640 mm
Metric Quad Crown	768×1008 mm
Metric Quad Large Crown	816×1056 mm
Metric Quad Demy	888×1128 mm
Metric Quad Royal	960×1272 mm

Common Book Sizes (Trimmed)

Crown Octavo	$7^5/_{16} \times 4^{13}/_{16}$ ins.
Large Crown Octavo	$7\frac{3}{4} \times 5^1/_{16}$ ins.
Demy Octavo	$8\frac{1}{2} \times 5^7/_{16}$ ins.
Royal Octavo	$9^3/_{16} \times 6\frac{1}{8}$ ins.
Metric Crown Octavo	186×123 mm
Metric Large Crown Octavo	198×129 mm
Metric Demy Octavo	213×138 mm
Metric Royal Octavo	234×156 mm

Royal Quarto	$12\frac{1}{2} \times 10$
Imperial Quarto	15×11
Crown Folio	15×10
Demy Folio	$17\frac{1}{2} \times 11\frac{1}{4}$
Royal Folio	$20 \times 12\frac{1}{2}$

Thermometer Readings

The three systems for marking thermometers are Centigrade, Fahrenheit and Réaumur. Centigrade, which shows 0° for freezing and 100° for boiling water, is used throughout the world for scientific purposes; it is used for general purposes in Europe. Fahrenheit, in which 32° is the freezing temperature and 212° the boiling temperature of water, is the scale previously used in Britain (now transferring to Centigrade) and still employed in the United States. Réaumur, with 0° for freezing and 80° for boiling water, is nearly obsolete, but is occasionally found in old books of European origin on scientific matters and cookery.

A comparison of Centigrade and Fahrenheit scales follows:

Centigrade		Fahrenheit
—40	=	—40
—30	=	—22
—25	=	—13
—20	=	—4
—17.8	=	0
—15	=	5
—10	=	14
—5	=	23
0	=	32
5	=	41
10	=	50
15	=	59
20	=	68
25	=	77

30	=	86
35	=	95
40	=	104
45	=	113
50	=	122
55	=	131
60	=	140
70	=	158
80	=	176
90	=	194
100	=	212

To change Centigrade to Fahrenheit, multiply by 9, divide by 5 and add 32.

To change Fahrenheit to Centigrade, subtract 32, multiply by 5 and divide by 9.

Normal blood temperature in human beings in 98.4° Fahrenheit.

Roman Numerals

I =	1		XVI =	16
II =	2		XVII =	17
III =	3		XVIII =	18
IV =	4		XIX =	19
V =	5		XX =	20
VI =	6		XXX =	30
VII =	7		XL =	40
VIII =	8		L =	50
IX =	9		LX =	60
X =	10		LXX =	70
XI =	11		LXXX =	80
XII =	12		XC =	90
XIII =	13		C =	100
XIV =	14		CC =	200
XV =	15		CCC =	300

```
   CD =    400          MV =    4,000
    D =    500           V =    5,000
  DCC =    700           X =   10,000
 DCCC =    800           L =   50,000
   CM =    900           C =  100,000
    M =  1,000           D =  500,000
MCMLX =  1,960           M = 1,000,000
   MM =  2,000
  MMM =  3,000
```

Common Formulae

Circumference of Circle	=	$2\pi r$ ($\pi = 3.1416$; r = radius)
Area of Circle	=	πr^2
Volume of Sphere	=	$\frac{1}{3}\pi r^3$
Surface of Sphere	=	$4\pi^2$
Volume of Cylinder	=	$\pi r^2 h$ (h = height)

Specific Gravity

Glass	=	2.4—2.6
Brass	=	8.1—8.6
Iron	=	8.95
Copper	=	8.95
Silver	=	10.3—10.5
Mercury	=	13.596

Coefficients of Expansion

Glass	=	0.000022
Iron	=	0.000033—0.000044
Copper	=	0.000051
Brass	=	0.000053—0.000057
Gases	=	0.00366

130

Boiling Points at 760 mm Pressure

Nitrous Oxide	—87.90°C
Chlorine	—33.60°C
Ammonia	—33.50°C
Ether	33.00°C
Chloroform	60.20°C
Alcohol	78.30°C
Benzene	80.40°C
Distilled Water	100.00°C
Sulphuric Acid	325.00°C
Mercury	357.25°C
Sulphur	444.70°C

Speed of Sound

Medium	Feet per Second
Through Air at 0°C	1,090
Through Water	4,758
Through Carbon Dioxide	850
Through Hydrogen	4,160
Through Glass	approx. 16,500

Chemical Names of Everyday Substances

Substance	Chemical Name
Alcohol	Ethyl Alcohol
Alum	Aluminium Potassium Sulphate
Baking Powder	Sodium Bicarbonate
Boracic Acid	Boric Acid
Borax	Sodium Borate
Chalk	Calcium Carbonate
Common Salt	Sodium Chloride
Epsom Salts	Magnesium Sulphate

131

Fire-damp	Methane
Glauber Salts	Sodium Sulphate
Hypo	Sodium Thiosulphate
Lime	Calcium Oxide
Magnesia	Magnesium Oxide
Plaster of Paris	Calcium Sulphate
Red Lead	Triplumbic Tetroxide
Sal Ammoniac	Ammonium Chloride
Saltpetre	Potassium Nitrate
Salts of Lemon	Potassium Hydrogen Oxalate
Sal Volatile	Ammonium Carbonate
Spirits of Salts	Hydrochloric Acid
Vinegar	Dilute Acetic Acid
Washing Soda	Crystalline Sodium Carbonate
White Lead	Basic Lead Carbonate

Table of Elements

Atomic No.	Element	Symbol	Atomic Weight
1	Hydrogen	H	1.008
2	Helium	He	4.003
3	Lithium	Li	6.94
4	Beryllium	Be	9.013
5	Boron	B	10.82
6	Carbon	C	12.01
7	Nitrogen	N	14.008
8	Oxygen	O	16.00
9	Fluorine	F	19.00
10	Neon	Ne	20.183
11	Sodium	Na	22.997
12	Magnesium	Mg	24.32
13	Aluminium	Al	26.97
14	Silicon	Si	28.06
15	Phosphorus	P	30.975

16	Sulphur	S	32.066
17	Chlorine	Cl	35.457
18	Argon	A	39.944
19	Potassium	K	39.096
20	Calcium	Ca	40.08
21	Scandium	Sc	45.10
22	Titanium	Ti	47.90
23	Vanadium	V	50.95
24	Chromium	Cr	52.01
25	Manganese	Mn	54.93
26	Iron	Fe	55.85
27	Cobalt	Co	58.94
28	Nickel	Ni	58.69
29	Copper	Cu	63.57
30	Zinc	Zn	65.38
31	Gallium	Ga	69.72
32	Germanium	Ge	72.60
33	Arsenic	As	74.91
34	Selenium	Se	78.96
35	Bromine	Br	79.916
36	Krypton	Kr	83.70
37	Rubidium	Rb	85.48
38	Strontium	Sr	87.63
39	Yttrium	Y	88.92
40	Zirconium	Zr	91.22
41	Niobium	Nb	92.91
42	Molybdenum	Mo	95.95
43	Technetium	Tc	98.00
44	Ruthenium	Ru	101.70
45	Rhodium	Rh	102.91
46	Palladium	Pd	106.70
47	Silver	Ag	107.88
48	Cadmium	Cd	112.41
49	Indium	In	114.76
50	Tin	Sn	118.70
51	Antimony	Sb	121.76

52	Tellurium	Te	127.61
53	Iodine	I	126.91
54	Xenon	Xe	131.30
55	Caesium	Cs	132.91
56	Barium	Ba	137.36
57	Lanthanum	La	138.92
58	Cerium	Ce	140.13
59	Praseodymium	Pr	140.92
60	Neodymium	Nd	144.27
61	Promethium	Pm	146.00
62	Samarium	Sm	150.43
63	Europium	Eu	152.00
64	Gadolinium	Gd	156.90
65	Terbium	Tb	159.20
66	Dysprosium	Dy	162.46
67	Holmium	Ho	164.94
68	Erbium	Er	167.20
69	Thulium	Tm	169.40
70	Ytterbium	Yb	173.04
71	Lutetium	Lu	174.99
72	Hafnium	Hf	178.60
73	Tantalum	Ta	180.88
74	Tungsten	W	183.92
75	Rhenium	Re	186.31
76	Osmium	Os	190.20
77	Iridium	Ir	193.10
78	Platinum	Pt	195.23
79	Gold	Au	197.20
80	Mercury	Hg	200.61
81	Thallium	Tl	204.39
82	Lead	Pb	207.21
83	Bismuth	Bi	209.00
84	Polonium	Po	210.00
85	Astatine	At	210.00
86	Radon	Rn	222.00
87	Francium	Fr	223.00

88	Radium	Ra	226.05
89	Actinium	Ac	227.00
90	Thorium	Th	232.12
91	Protoactinium	Pa	231.00
92	Uranium	U	238.07
93	Neptunium	Np	237.00
94	Plutonium	Pl	238.00
95	Americium	Am	243.00
96	Curium	Cm	245.00
97	Berkelium	Bk	249.00
98	Californium	Cf	249.00
99	Einsteinium	E	255.00
100	Fermium	Fm	255.00
101	Mendelevium	Mv	256.00

Chemical Indicators

Indicators show whether a substance is alkaline, acid or neutral. The following list gives the effect of adding an indicator.

Indicator	Alkaline	Acid	Neutral
Litmus	turns blue	turns red	turns purple
Methyl Orange	turns yellow	turns pink	remains orange

Wind Force

When weather forecasters want to inform ships of the exact strength of winds likely to blow in their areas, they do so by using the Beaufort Scale, referring to 'Force 2' or 'Force 5', or whatever is appropriate. The Scale is given overleaf...

Force Number	Description	M. P. H.
0	Calm	0— 1
1	Light air	1— 3
2	Slight breeze	4— 7
3	Gentle breeze	8— 12
4	Moderate breeze	13— 18
5	Fresh breeze	19— 24
6	Strong breeze	25— 31
7	High wind	32— 38
8	Gale	39— 46
9	Strong gale	47— 54
10	Whole gale	55— 63
11	Storm	64— 72
12	Hurricane	73— 82
13		83— 92
14		93—103
15		104—114
16		115—125
17		126—136

PEOPLE AND THE ARTS

Nowadays most of us are a little inclined to forget the importance of the arts in adding enjoyment and beauty to our lives and in shaping the world in which we live. Many people are inclined to dismiss great paintings as 'a lot of dry and dusty old pieces of canvas in museums', although the art of the great painters in the past has given us our skill in present-day industrial design, our knowledge of colours and our ability to make our own homes pleasant to look at and pleasant to live in.

Here are some of the leading artists, sculptors, musicians and writers of the past:

ADAM, *Robert (1728—1792).* Scottish architect who helped revive the handsome building styles of ancient Greece. Much of his work can still be seen in central London and in Edinburgh, where a large proportion of the 'New Town' was erected according to his designs. He was also a leading interior decorator, and rooms designed by him are very much prized today.

ADDISON, *Joseph (1672—1719).* Leading writer and politician. He is remembered today as a writer of light and amusing essays for the journal called the *Spectator,* which he founded in partnership with Sir Richard Steele. These essays are regarded as some of the finest examples of English writing.

AESCHYLUS *(525—456 B.C.).* One of the leading playwrights of ancient Greece, he is regarded as the father of Greek tragedy. His plays have been translated into English and make interesting reading.

AESOP *(629—560 B.C.).* Greek slave who compiled a large collection of moral fables, many of which are as applicable today as they were when first told.

ANGELICO, Fra *(1387—1455)*. One of the greatest Italian Renaissance painters. Many of his finest pictures are in the galleries at Florence.

ARISTOPHANES *(450—385 B.C.)*. Leading playwright of ancient Greece. Most of his plays are satirical and are still widely read and performed.

AUSTEN, *Jane (1775—1817)*, English novelist. Wrote six books, *Sense and Sensibility, Pride and Prejudice, Northanger Abbey, Mansfield Park, Emma* and *Persuasion,* which are among the greatest novels in the English language. They have seldom been 'out of print' since they were first published.

BACH, *Johann Sebastian (1685—1750)*. German composer and organist; was one of the founders of his country's tradition of orchestral music. Among his works are the *Mass in B Minor,* the *St. Matthew Passion* and many cantatas and works for the organ.

BACON, *Francis (1561—1626)*. Leading English politician during the reigns of Queen Elizabeth I and King James I, but it is as an author that he is largely remembered. His best-known works are his *Novum Organum* and his *Essays.*

BALZAC, *Honoré de (1799—1850)*. French novelist, famous for his penetrating studies of the society of his time. Among his best-known novels are *Le Père Goriot* and *La Cousine Bette.*

BEETHOVEN, *Ludwig van (1770—1827)*. German composer, famous in particular for his symphonies. By the age of thirty he was nearly deaf, though much of his great music was written after this time.

BERLIOZ, *Hector (1803—1869)*. French composer of symphonies, operas and songs. His best known symphonic work is *Romeo and Juliet.*

BIZET, *Georges (1838—1875)*. French composer of operas, including *The Pearl-Fishers* and *Carmen,* which is one of the world's most popular operas.

BLAKE, *William (1757—1827)*. British poet and artist; author of many religious works, among them the *Prophetic Books* from which the popular hymn 'Jerusalem' is taken.

BOTTICELLI, *Sandro (1444—1510).* Italian Renaissance painter of the Florentine school. His greatest works are in art galleries in Florence.

BRAHMS, *Johannes (1833—1897).* German composer, whose works include several major symphonies, sonatas and much piano music popular with concert audiences.

BRONTË, *Sisters: Charlotte (1816—1855), Emily (1818—1848)* and *Anne (1820—1849).* English novelists. Charlotte's books include *Jane Eyre, Shirley* and *Villette;* Emily wrote *Wuthering Heights;* Anne's two books were *Agnes Grey* and *The Tenant of Wildfell Hall.* Of these, *Jane Eyre* and *Wuthering Heights* are the most widely read today.

BROWNING, *Elizabeth Barrett (1806—1861).* English poet, and wife of poet Robert Browning. She is best known for her sonnets.

BROWNING, *Robert (1812—1889).* English poet. Some of his best known works are *Paracelsus, Sordello* and *The Ring and the Book.*

BRUEGHEL, *Pieter, the Elder (1520—1569).* Flemish painter; one of the greatest of his period and founder of a school of artists.

BURNS, *Robert (1759—1796).* Scottish poet, famous for such poems as *Tam o' Shanter* and *The Cotter's Saturday Night* and for such popular songs as *Auld Lang Syne.*

BYRON, *George Gordon, Lord (1788—1824).* English poet, whose work has remained constantly 'in print' for a century and a half. He died in Greece, to which he had gone to aid the Greeks in their struggle for independence.

CÉZANNE, *Paul (1839—1906).* One of the greatest of the French Post-Impressionist painters. Like many of his contemporaries, he was not fully appreciated as an artist during his lifetime.

CHAUCER, *Geoffrey (1340—1400).* One of the greatest of English poets. His *Canterbury Tales* are widely read and enjoyed today.

CHEKHOV, *Anton (1860—1904).* Russian writer of short

stories and plays. Among his best-known works are the plays *The Cherry Orchard, The Three Sisters* and *Uncle Vanya*.

CHIPPENDALE, *Thomas (c. 1718—1779).* English furniture designer, who set the pattern for the furnishing of thousands of British households. Surviving examples of his work sell for many hundreds of pounds.

CHOPIN, *Frédéric (1810—1849).* Polish composer and musician, famed for his piano compositions. It was a phrase of his music, broadcast over and over again by Warsaw Radio in 1939, which signalled to the world that the Polish Army was still holding out against the invading Germans.

COLERIDGE, *Samuel Taylor (1772—1834).* Poet, philosopher and critic. In the first rank of English poets. Some of his best-known works are *Kubla Khan, The Ancient Mariner* and *Christabel.*

COLERIDGE-TAYLOR, *Samuel (1785—1912).* British composer and violinist, best remembered for his cantata *Hiawatha.*

DANTE ALIGHIERI *(1265—1321).* Italy's greatest poet. He was also a soldier and politician and at one time was sentenced to be burned at the stake for his political allegiance. His greatest work is the *Divina Commedia.*

DA VINCI, *Leonardo (1452—1519).* Florentine painter and scientist. He produced plans for a submarine and an aeroplane, among other things, four centuries before they became practical engineering possibilities. His best-known painting is the world-famous *Mona Lisa.*

DEBUSSY, *Claude Achille (1862—1918).* French composer; wrote many well-known piano pieces, including *Clair de Lune.* He was a major influence on 20th c. music.

DEGAS, *(Hilaire Germain) Edgar (1834—1917).* French Impressionist painter, famous for his studies of ballet dancers.

DICKENS, *Charles (1812—1870).* Leading English novelist, who is still widely read. His best-known works include *David Copperfield, Oliver Twist, The Pickwick Papers, Great Expectations* and *A Christmas Carol.*

DOSTOEVSKY, *Fyodor (1821—1881).* Russian novelist, whose work has had much influence on subsequent writing. Among his best-known novels are *Crime and Punishment, The Idiot* and *The Brothers Karamazov.*

DUMAS, *Alexandre (1802—1870).* French novelist and dramatist. His best-remembered novels are *The Three Musketeers* and *Twenty Years After.* His son Alexandre (1824—1895) was also an author and playwright.

ELGAR, *Sir Edward (1857—1934).* English composer; wrote 'Land of Hope and Glory' as part of the *Pomp and Circumstance* march. His *Enigma Variations* is a popular concert work, and he also wrote the oratorio, *The Dream of Gerontius,* and the symphonic study *Falstaff.*

EURIPIDES *(c. 484—407 B.C.).* Greek dramatist, famous for his tragedies, only a few of which survive. Among the best known are *Alcestis, Medea* and *The Trojan Women.*

FLAUBERT, *Gustave (1821—1880).* French author, well known for his novel *Madame Bovary.*

GAUGUIN, *Paul (1848—1903).* French painter, renowned for his pictures of life in the Pacific Islands.

GIOTTO *(1267—1337).* Italian painter, considered the first painter whose work truly belonged to the Renaissance rather than the Middle Ages.

GOETHE, *Johann Wolfgang von (1749—1832).* German poet; the most famous of his works is his play *Faust.* In German writing he takes much the same position as Shakespeare in the history of English literature and drama. He was also a scientist of considerable importance.

GOGOL, *Nikolai Vasilievich (1809—1852).* Russian novelist and dramatist. His best-known works are his novel *Dead Souls* and his play *The Government Inspector.*

GORKY, *Maxim (1868—1936).* Russian novelist and dramatist. His best-known works are the novels *Mother* and *Comrades,* and the play *The Lower Depths.*

GOUNOD, *Charles Francois (1818—1893).* French composer, well known for his opera *Faust.*

GOYA Y LUCIENTES, *Francisco (1746—1828).* Spanish painter and official Court artist. Although most of his works are in Spain, several paintings can be seen in the National Gallery in London.

GRECO, EL *(1542—1614).* The correct name of this Spanish artist was Domenico Theotocopouli, but his associations with the island of Crete led to the name 'El Greco'. His paintings and sculpture were religious in character.

HANDEL, *George Frederick (1685—1759).* Composer; German-born, but became a British subject. He wrote nearly fifty operas and many oratorios, including *The Messiah.*

HARDY, *Thomas (1840—1928).* English poet and novelist. Among his best-known novels are *Tess of the d'Urbervilles, Far from the Madding Crowd, The Mayor of Casterbridge, The Return of the Native* and *Jude the Obscure.*

HAYDN, *Franz Joseph (1732—1809).* Austrian composer of many symphonies, operas, oratorios and anthems. His oratorios *The Creation* and *The Seasons* are performed frequently.

HOGARTH, *William (1697—1764).* English painter, best remembered for his satirical cartoons of eighteenth-century life and manners in England.

HOLBEIN, *Hans, the Younger (1497—1543).* German portrait painter, several of whose pictures are in the National Gallery in London. His painting of the family of King Henry VII was lost in the Great Fire of London, but much of his work remains.

HOMER *(c. 850 B.C.?).* Probably born in Greece, he was the author of two great works, *The Iliad* and *The Odyssey.*

JOHNSON, *Samuel (1709—1784).* English poet, essayist and lexicographer. Much information regarding him comes to us by way of his biographer, James Boswell.

JONSON, *Ben (1572—1637).* English dramatist, famous for such comedies as *Volpone* and *The Alchemist.*

JOYCE, *James (1882—1941).* Irish author; spent most of his life in Italy, Switzerland and France. His best-known works are *A Portrait of the Artist as a Young Man, Ulysses* and *Finnegan's Wake*.

KEATS, *John (1795—1821).* English poet; wrote for only about five years, but his outstanding work had a tremendous influence on later poets. Among his best-remembered writings are *Endymion, The Eve of St Agnes, Ode on a Grecian Urn* and *Ode to a Nightingale.*

LAWRENCE, *David Herbert (1885—1930).* English novelist and poet; also wrote a number of penetrating travel essays. His leading novels include *Sons and Lovers, Aaron's Rod, The Rainbow* and *Women in Love.*

LISZT, *Franz (1811—1886).* Hungarian pianist and composer. His piano music, including the *Hungarian Rhapsodies,* is often heard at concerts.

MANET, *Édouard (1832—1883).* French Impressionist painter; was one of the first painters to use colour to express light and shadow.

MARLOWE, *Christopher (1564—1593).* English dramatist and poet, whose work undoubtedly influenced Shakespeare's early plays. His best-known plays are *Dr Faustus, Tamburlaine* and *The Jew of Malta.*

MATISSE, *Henri (1869—1954).* French painter. One of the leading artists of the modern schools, he was known especially for his use of pure colour and for his intricate compositions.

MAUPASSANT, *Guy de (1850—1893).* French writer, famous for his short stories.

MELVILLE, *Herman (1819—1891).* American novelist, many of whose writings dealt with the sea. His best-known books are *Moby Dick, Billy Budd* and *Typee.*

MENDELSSOHN-BARTHOLDY, *Jakob Ludwig Felix (1809—1847).* German composer, whose works are often played. Among his best-loved compositions are the oratorio *Elijah,* the *'Scotch' Symphony,* the *'Italian' Symphony* and the overture *Fingal's Cave.*

MICHELANGELO BUONAROTTI *(1475—1564).* Italian sculptor, architect and painter. The most famous of the

Florentine artists, he painted the frescoes in the Sistine Chapel in Rome.

MILTON, *John (1608—1674).* One of the greatest English poets. Among his best-known works are *Paradise Lost, Samson Agonistes* and *Areopagitica.*

MOLIÈRE *(Jean Baptiste Poquelin) (1622—1673).* Leading French dramatist. His most popular plays include *Tartuffe, Le Bourgeois Gentilhomme* and *L'École des Maris.*

MOZART, *Wolfgang Amadeus (1756—1791).* Austrian composer. His most popular works include the operas *The Magic Flute* and *The Marriage of Figaro,* and many symphonies, concerti and string quartets.

OFFENBACH, *Jacques (1819—1880).* German composer of light operas. These include the often performed *Tales of Hoffmann.*

OVID *(43 B.C.—A.D.17).* Roman poet; author of the *Heroides,* the *Amores,* the *Metamorphoses* and many other works which are read both in Latin and in translation.

PROUST, *Marcel (1871—1922).* French novelist, famed for his series of novels *A la Recherche du Temps Perdu.*

PUCCINI, *Giacomo (1858—1924).* Italian composer of many popular operas, including *La Bohème* and *Madame Butterfly.*

PURCELL, *Henry (1658—1695).* English composer. He wrote much fine church music, including chants for psalms, while organist at London's Westminster Abbey.

PUSHKIN, *Alexander (1799—1837).* Russian poet and writer of stories. One of his most famous short stories is *The Queen of Spades.*

RACHMANINOV, *Sergei Vassilievich (1873—1943).* Russian composer and pianist; wrote many popular concert works and also several operas.

RACINE, *Jean (1639—1699).* Leading French tragic dramatist. His best-known plays include *Phédre* and *Andromaque.*

RAPHAEL, *Sanzio (1483—1520).* One of the greatest

144

Italian painters of the Renaissance. His works are found in art galleries throughout the world.

REMBRANDT, *Harmensz van Rijn (1606—1669).* Dutch artist; one of the world's greatest portrait painters. Some of his work can be seen in London's National Gallery.

RENOIR, *Pierre Auguste (1841—1919).* French Impressionist painter, famous in particular for his studies of women. His works appear in galleries all over the world.

REYNOLDS, *Sir Joshua (1723—1792).* The first President of the Royal Academy and the greatest English portrait painter of his day.

ROSSINI, *Gioacchino Antonio (1793—1868).* Italian operatic composer, best known for *The Barber of Seville* and *William Tell.*

ROUSSEAU, *Jean Jacques (1712—1778).* French writer and philosopher. His best-known writings include *Confessions, Émile* and *Le Contrat Social.*

RUBENS, *Peter Paul (1577—1640).* One of the best known and appreciated of the Flemish school of painters; he had much influence on later artists. His paintings are found in major art galleries all over the world.

SCHUBERT, *Franz Peter (1797—1828).* Austrian composer; died at the age of thirty-one. His many songs and his chamber music are very popular, as is his *Unfinished Symphony.*

SCHUMANN, *Robert (1810—1856).* German composer, renowned for his symphonies, chamber music and many major piano works.

SHAKESPEARE, *William (1564—1616).* English dramatist and poet, generally regarded as the world's greatest playwright. His wide range of tragedies, historical dramas and comedies has been performed more than the work of any other dramatist in history.

SHAW, *George Bernard (1856—1950).* Irish playwright and critic. Among his best-known plays are *Pygmalion, Caesar and Cleopatra, Man and Superman* and *Saint Joan.*

SHELLEY, *Percy Bysshe (1792—1822).* English poet. In his

145

day he was considered revolutionary; today he is regarded as a poetic genius. Among his best-known writings are *Adonais, Prometheus Unbound* and *To a Skylark.*

SIBELIUS, *Jean (1865—1957).* Finnish composer, renowned for his tone-poems, particularly *Finlandia.*

STENDHAL *(Henri Beyle) (1783—1842).* French novelist; author of *Le Rouge et le Noir* and *La Chartreuse de Parme.*

STEVENSON, *Robert Louis (1850—1894).* English novelist and poet, author of *Treasure Island, Kidnapped, The Strange Case of Dr Jekyll and Mr Hyde* and many other widely read books.

STRAUSS, *Johann, the Younger (1825—1899).* Austrian composer. His best-known works include the *Blue Danube Waltz* and *Tales from the Vienna Woods,* and the opera *Die Fledermaus.*

STRAUSS, *Richard (1864—1949).* German composer, best known for such operas as *Der Rosenkavalier* and *Elektra* and such compositions as *Till Eulenspiegel.*

SWIFT, *Jonathan (1667—1745).* English satirist, author of *Gulliver's Travels.*

TCHAIKOWSKY, *Peter Ilyich (1840—1893).* Russian composer of symphonic, operatic and ballet music, including *Swan Lake, Nutcracker Suite* and *The Sleeping Beauty.* Among his most popular works are the *1812 Overture* and the Fifth and Sixth symphonies.

TENNYSON, *Alfred, Lord (1809—1892).* English poet. He was made Poet Laureate for his consistently high standard of work over many years. His greatest verses, such as *The Idylls of the King,* had medieval England as their subject.

TITIAN *(c. 1477—1576).* The greatest painter of the Venetian school. Among his best-known portraits are those of Charles V, and Pope Paul III. His paintings of religious and mythological subjects are particularly briliant.

TOLSTOY, *Leo Nikolayevich, Count (1828—1910).* Russian novelist, two of whose works, *War and Peace* and *Anna Karenina,* are considered among the greatest novels of all time.

TURNER, *Joseph Mallord William (1775—1851).* English painter, famous for his seascapes and landscapes in which he devoted himself to the study of light, using brilliant, luminous colour.

TWAIN, *Mark (Samuel Langhorne Clemens) (1835—1910).* American novelist; author of *Tom Sawyer, Huckleberry Finn, The Prince and the Pauper* and *Pudd'nhead Wilson.*

VAN DYCK, *Sir Anthony (1599—1641).* Flemish portrait painter, appointed Court painter to King Charles I of England.

VAN GOGH, *Vincent (1853—1890).* Dutch painter, who in a short period of seven years as an artist produced vividly coloured canvases which are known and loved throughout the world.

VELASQUEZ, *Diego Rodriguez de Silva y (1599—1660).* Spanish portrait painter, famous in particular for his Court paintings such as *Las Meninas (The Maids of Honour).* His work influenced the development of modern painting.

VERDI, *Giuseppe (1813—1901).* Italian composer of church and operatic music. He wrote a number of operas which are widely performed, such as *Aida, Rigoletto* and *La Traviata.*

VERMEER, VAN DELFT, *Jan (1632—1675).* Dutch painter of portraits and landscapes, famed for his beautiful studies of light and its effects.

VERONESE, *Paolo (1528—1588).* Italian painter of the Veronese and Venetian Schools. His pictures are remarkable for their colouring.

VIRGIL *(70—19 B.C.).* Considered the greatest of all the Roman poets. His major work is the unfinished *Aeneid,* based on the story of the settlement of Aeneas in Italy after the destruction of Troy.

VOLTAIRE *(François Marie Arouet) (1694—1778).* French writer and satirist. Among his leading works are *Candide* and the *Dictionnaire Philosophique.*

WAGNER, *Richard (1813—1883).* German composer, whose operas, revolutionary in style in their day, include *Die*

Walküre, Lohengrin, Die Meistersinger and *Tristan und Isolde*.

WOOLF, *Virginia (1882—1941).* English novelist and critic. Among her best-known novels are *Mrs Dalloway, To the Lighthouse* and *The Waves*.

WORDSWORTH, *William (1770—1850).* English poet, noted for his supreme mastery of language. Was made Poet Laureate in 1843.

WREN, *Sir Christopher (1632—1723).* English architect-scientist. Was called upon by Charles II to plan repairs to old St Paul's Cathedral, but before these could be carried out the Cathedral was gutted in the Great Fire of London, and his work became that of designing the present Cathedral. He also designed more than fifty other churches.

YEATS, *William Butler (1865—1939).* Irish poet. One of the great poets of recent times, he was awarded the Nobel Prize for Literature in 1923.

PEOPLE AND SPORT

What is the purpose of sport? Is it records, results or simply the most enjoyable method of keeping healthy? Nobody can give the complete answer, but it is probably a combination of all three.

Every sport has its own story—usually a fascinating history and an origin far back in time. In the following pages you will find brief histories of some of the most popular sports, with their principal facts and figures.

Athletics

The first great athletes were the Greeks, who held Olympic Games more than two thousand seven hundred years ago. These Games were a regular feature of Greek life for more than a thousand years, but when the Romans abolished them, in 394 A.D., athletics became almost a forgotten art for many centuries. It was not until about two hundred years ago that cross-country running for wagers renewed interest in the sport. By the eighteen-fifties most schools and athletic teams and the universities held their own championships. The standards were low, however, compared with those of the present day. It took seventy years to push the high-jump record from six feet to seven feet, and long-distance runners of today have clipped many minutes off the best times ever recorded by their grandfathers.

It was the revival of the Olympic Games in 1896 that made athletics a sport for the millions, for the appeal of international competition is greater than any other.

Here are some of the world's most recent records:

Running

Event	Holder	Nation	Record	Year
100 m	J. Hines	USA	9.9 s	1968
	R. Smith	USA	9.9 s	1968
	C. Greene	USA	9.9 s	1968
	E. Hart	USA	9.9 s	1968
	R. Robinson	USA	9.9 s	1972
200 m	T. Smith	USA	19.8 s	1968
	D. Quarrie	Jamaica	19.8 s	1971
400 m	L. Evans	USA	43.8 s	1968
800 m	P. Snell	N. Zealand	1 min 44.3 s	1962
	R. Doubell	Australia	1 min 44.3 s	1968
	D. Wottle	USA	1 min 44.3 s	1972
1,500 m	J. Ryun	USA	3 min 33.1 s	1967
5,000 m	R. Clarke	Australia	13 min 16.6 s	1966
10,000 m	R. Clarke	Australia	27 min 39.4 s	1965
Marathon	D. Clayton	Australia	2 hr 08 min 33.6 s	1969

Field Events

	Holder	Nation	Record	Year
High Jump	P. Matzdorf	U.S.A.	7 ft. 6¼ in	1971
Pole Vault	R. Seagren	U.S.A.	18 ft. 5¾ in	1972
Long Jump	R. Beamon	U.S.A.	29 ft. 2½ in	1968
Triple Jump	P. Perez	Cuba	57 ft. 1 in	1971
Putting the Shot	R. Matson	U.S.A.	71 ft. 5½ in	1967
Discus	J. Silvester	U.S.A.	224 ft. 5 in	1968
	R. Bruch	Sweden	224 ft. 5 in	1972
Hammer	W. Schmidt	Germany	250 ft. 8 in	1971
Javelin	J. Lusis	U.S.S.R.	307 ft. 9 in	1972
Decathalon	W. Toomey	U.S.A.	8,417 pts	1969
20 km walk	P. Nihill	Gt. Britain	1 hr 24 min 50 s	1972
50 km walk	B. Kannenberg	Germany	3 hr 52 min 45 s	1972

Hurdles

Event	Holder	Nation	Record	Year
110 m	M. Lauer	Germany	13.2 s	1959
	L. Calhoun	U.S.A.	13.2 s	1960
	E. McCulloch	U.S.A.	13.2 s	1967
400 m	D. Hemery	Gt. Britain	48.1 s	1968
3,000 m Steeplechase	K. O'Brien	Australia	8 min. 22.0 s	1970

Cycling

Since the bicycle craze of the 1 880 s, cycle-racing speeds have steadily improved. Unfortunately, the value of world records has been reduced by the complexity of the ways in which they can be set up, such as *unpaced, standing start, flying start, human paced* and *motor cycle paced*. Here is a selection of the more outstanding records:

Event	Holder	Record	Venue	Year
1 km	R. Harris	1 m. 8.6 s	Milan	1952
5 km	O. Ritter	5 m. 51.6 s	Mexico	1968
10 km	O. Ritter	11 m. 58.4 s	Mexico	1968
1 hour	O. Ritter	30.225 m	Mexico	1968

Land's End to John O'Groats (870 miles) was covered by Dick Poole in 1 day, 23 hours and 46 minutes in 1965. Land's End to John O'Groats feminine record was set up by Mrs. Eileen Sheridan in 2 days, 11 hours and 7 minutes in 1954.

151

Football

The history of football may date as far back as Roman times, when men of the army probably played *harpastum*, a Roman game remarkably like modern Rugby Football. In the sixteenth century the game was played in England by whole villages, often with as many as a hundred men on each side. Injuries were numerous and severe, and the game was extremely dangerous until the early part of the last century when many schools in England improved it and set up codes of rules. These became standardised in the eighteen-sixties, when those who favoured 'the handling game' formed the Rugby Union and those who preferred non-handling established the Football Association. There are now seven distinct forms of football, but the three most widely played are Association (eleven players, world wide), Rugby Union (fifteen players; Britain, France, Australia, New Zealand, South Africa) and Rugby League (thirteen players; Britain, France, Australia, New Zealand).

Association Football

The world record crowd at an Association Football match was 200,000 at the World Cup Final of 1950, between Brazil and Uruguay in Rio de Janeiro. The highest score in a match recognised as official was Arbroath 36, Bon Accord 0, in a Scottish Cup match in 1885. The highest score in an international match was England 17, Australia O, at Sydney in 1951.

World Cup Winners

1930 Uruguay	1958 Brazil
1934 Italy	1962 Brazil
1938 Italy	1966 England
1950 Uruguay	1970 Brazil
1954 West Germany	

F. A. Cup Winners

1873—4	Oxford University
1874—5	Royal Engineers
1875—6	Wanderers
1876—7	Wanderers
1877—8	Wanderers
1878—9	Old Etonians
1879—80	Clapham Rovers
1880—1	Old Carthusians
1881—2	Old Etonians
1882—3	Blackburn Olympic
1883—4	Blackburn Rovers
1884—5	Blackburn Rovers
1885—6	Blackburn Rovers
1886—7	Aston Villa
1887—8	West Bromwich Albion
1888—9	Preston N. E.
1889—90	Blackburn Rovers
1890—1	Blackburn Rovers
1891—2	West Bromwich Albion
1892—3	Wolverhampton Wanderers
1893—4	Notts County
1894—5	Aston Villa
1895—6	Sheffield Wednesday
1896—7	Aston Villa
1897—8	Nottingham Forest
1898—9	Sheffield United
1899—1900	Bury
1900—1	Tottenham H.
1901—2	Sheffield United
1902—3	Bury
1903—4	Manchester City
1904—5	Aston Villa
1905—6	Everton
1906—7	Sheffield Wednesday
1907—8	Wolverhampton Wanderers
1908—9	Manchester United
1909—10	Newcastle United
1910—11	Bradford City
1911—12	Barnsley
1912—13	Aston Villa
1913—14	Burnley
1914—15	Sheffield United
1915—19	*No competition*
1919—20	Aston Villa
1920—1	Tottenham H.
1921—2	Huddersfield T.
1922—3	Bolton Wanderers
1923—4	Newcastle United
1924—5	Sheffield United
1925—6	Bolton Wanderers

1926—7	Cardiff City	1952—3	Blackpool
1927—8	Blackburn Rovers	1953—4	West Bromwich Albion
1928—9	Bolton Wanderers		
1929—30	Arsenal	1954—5	Newcastle United
1930—1	West Bromwich Albion	1955—6	Manchester City
		1956—7	Aston Villa
1931—2	Newcastle United	1957—8	Bolton Wanderers
1932—3	Everton	1958—9	Nottingham Forest
1933—4	Manchester City		
1934—5	Sheffield Wednesday	1959—60	Wolverhampton Wanderers
1935—6	Arsenal	1960—1	Tottenham H.
1936—7	Sunderland	1961—2	Tottenham H.
1937—8	Preston N. E.	1962—3	Manchester United
1938—9	Portsmouth	1963—4	West Ham United
1939—45	*No competition*		
1945—6	Derby County	1964—5	Liverpool
1946—7	Charlton Athletic	1965—6	Everton
1947—8	Manchester United	1966—7	Tottenham H.
		1967—8	West Bromwich Albion
1948—9	Wolverhampton Wanderers		
		1968—9	Manchester City
1949—50	Arsenal	1969—70	Chelsea
1950—1	Newcastle United	1970—71	Arsenal
1951—2	Newcastle United	1971—72	Leeds United

1. Football League Champions (1st Division)

1890—1	Everton	1898—9	Aston Villa
1891—2	Sunderland	1899—1900	Aston Villa
1892—3	Sunderland		
1893—4	Aston Villa	1900—1	Liverpool
1894—5	Sunderland	1901—2	Sunderland
1895—6	Aston Villa	1902—3	Sheffield Wed.
1896—7	Aston Villa	1903—4	Sheffield Wednesday
1897—8	Sheffield United		

1904—5	Newcastle United	1938—9	Everton
1905—6	Liverpool	1939—46	*No competition*
1906—7	Newcastle United	1946—7	Liverpool
1907—8	Manchester United	1947—8	Arsenal
1908—9	Newcastle United	1948—9	Portsmouth
1909—10	Aston Villa	1949—50	Portsmouth
1910—11	Manchester United	1950—1	Tottenham Hotspur
1911—12	Blackburn Rovers		
1912—13	Sunderland	1951—2	Manchester United
1913—14	Blackburn Rovers		
1914—15	Everton	1952—3	Arsenal
1915—19	*No competition*	1953—4	Wolverhampton Wanderers
1919—20	West Bromwich Albion		
		1954—5	Chelsea
1920—1	Burnley	1955—6	Manchester United
1921—2	Liverpool		
1922—3	Liverpool	1956—7	Manchester United
1923—4	Huddersfield Town		
		1957—8	Wolverhampton Wanderers
1924—5	Huddersfield Town		
		1958—9	Wolverhampton Wanderers
1925—6	Huddersfield Town		
1926—7	Newcastle United	1959—60	Burnley
1927—8	Everton	1960—1	Tottenham Hotspur
1928—9	Sheffield Wednesday		
		1961—2	Ipswich
1929—30	Sheffield Wednesday	1962—3	Everton
		1963—4	Liverpool
1930—1	Arsenal	1964—5	Manchester United
1931—2	Everton	1965—6	Liverpool
1932—3	Arsenal	1966—7	Manchester United
1933—4	Arsenal	1967—8	Manchester City
1934—5	Arsenal	1968—9	Leeds
1935—6	Sunderland	1969—70	Everton
1936—7	Manchester City	1970—71	Arsenal
1937—8	Arsenal	1971—72	Derby County

155

2. Scottish Cup Winners

1875—6	Queen's Park
1876—7	Vale of Leven
1877—8	Vale of Leven
1878—9	Vale of Leven
1879—80	Queen's Park
1880—1	Queen's Park
1881—2	Queen's Park
1882—3	Dumbarton
1883—4	Queen's Park
1884—5	Renton
1885—6	Queen's Park
1886—7	Hibernian
1887—8	Renton
1888—9	Third Lanark
1889—90	Queen's Park
1890—1	Hearts
1891—2	Celtic
1892—3	Queen's Park
1893—4	Rangers
1894—5	St Bernard's
1895—6	Hearts
1896—7	Rangers
1897—8	Rangers
1898—9	Celtic
1899—1900	
	Celtic
1900—1	Hearts
1901—2	Hibernian
1902—3	Rangers
1903—4	Celtic
1904—5	Third Lanark
1905—6	Hearts
1906—7	Celtic
1907—8	Celtic
1908—9	*Cup withheld (riot)*
1909—10	Dundee
1910—11	Celtic
1911—12	Celtic
1912—13	Falkirk
1913—14	Celtic
1914—19	*No competition*
1919—20	Kilmarnock
1920—1	Patrick Thistle
1921—2	Morton
1922—3	Celtic
1923—4	Airdrieonians
1924—5	Celtic
1925—6	St Mirren
1926—7	Celtic
1927—8	Rangers
1928—9	Kilmarnock
1929—30	Rangers
1930—1	Celtic
1931—2	Rangers
1932—3	Celtic
1933—4	Rangers
1934—5	Rangers
1935—6	Rangers
1936—7	Celtic
1937—8	East Fife
1938—9	Clyde
1939—46	*No competition*
1946—7	Aberdeen
1947—8	Rangers
1948—9	Rangers
1949—50	Rangers
1950—1	Celtic
1951—2	Motherwell

1952—3	Rangers	1962—3	Rangers
1953—4	Celtic	1963—4	Rangers
1954—5	Clyde	1964—5	Celtic
1955—6	Hearts	1965—6	Rangers
1956—7	Falkirk	1966—7	Celtic
1957—8	Clyde	1967—8	Dunfermline
1958—9	St. Mirren	1968—9	Celtic
1959—60	Rangers	1969—70	Aberdeen
1960—1	Dunfermline	1970—71	Celtic
1961—2	Rangers	1971—72	Celtic

3. Scottish League Champions

1891—2	Dumbarton	1914—15	Celtic
1892—3	Celtic	1915—16	Celtic
1893—4	Celtic	1916—17	Celtic
1894—5	Hearts	1917—18	Rangers
1895—6	Celtic	1918—19	Celtic
1896—7	Hearts	1919—20	Rangers
1897—8	Celtic	1920—1	Rangers
1898—9	Rangers	1921—2	Celtic
1899—1900		1922—3	Rangers
	Rangers	1923—4	Rangers
1900—1	Rangers	1924—5	Rangers
1901—2	Rangers	1925—6	Celtic
1902—3	Hibernian	1926—7	Rangers
1903—4	Third Lanark	1927—8	Rangers
1904—5	Celtic	1928—9	Rangers
1905—6	Celtic	1929—30	Rangers
1906—7	Celtic	1930—1	Rangers
1907—8	Celtic	1931—2	Motherwell
1908—9	Celtic	1932—3	Rangers
1909—10	Celtic	1933—4	Rangers
1910—11	Rangers	1934—5	Rangers
1911—12	Rangers	1935—6	Celtic
1912—13	Rangers	1936—7	Rangers
1913—14	Celtic	1937—8	Celtic

1938—9	Rangers	1958—9	Rangers
1939—46	*No competition*	1959—60	Hearts
1946—7	Rangers	1960—1	Rangers
1947—8	Hibernian	1961—2	Dundee
1948—9	Rangers	1962—3	Rangers
1949—50	Rangers	1963—4	Rangers
1950—1	Hibernian	1964—5	Kilmarnock
1951—2	Hibernian	1965—6	Celtic
1952—3	Rangers	1966—7	Celtic
1953—4	Celtic	1967—8	Celtic
1954—5	Aberdeen	1968—9	Celtic
1955—6	Rangers	1969—70	Celtic
1956—7	Rangers	1970—71	Celtic
1957—8	Hearts	1971—72	Celtic

4. Home International Championship (since 1946)

1946—7	England	1960—1	England
1947—8	England	1961—2	Scotland
1948—9	Scotland	1962—3	Scotland
1949—50	England	1963—4	England, Scotland and Ireland
1950—1	Scotland		
1951—2	Wales-England	1964—5	England
1952—3	England-Scotland	1965—6	England
1953—4	England	1966—7	Scotland
1954—5	England	1967—8	England
1955—6	England, Scotland, Wales and Ireland	1968—9	England
		1969—70	England, Scotland and Wales
1956—7	England		
1957—8	England-Ireland	1970—71	England
1958—9	England-Ireland	1971—72	England, Scotland and Wales
1959—60	England, Wales and Scotland		

5. Rugby Union
International Championship (since 1946)

| 1946—7 | Wales and England | 1948—9 | Ireland |
| 1947—8 | Ireland | 1949—50 | Wales |

1950—1	Ireland	1960—1	France
1951—2	Wales	1961—2	France
1952—3	England	1962—3	England
1953—4	England, France and Wales	1963—4	Scotland and Wales
1954—5	Wales and France	1964—5	Wales
		1965—6	Wales
1955—6	Wales	1966—7	France
1956—7	England	1967—8	France
1957—8	England	1968—9	Wales
1958—9	France	1969—70	France
1959—60	England and France	1970—71	Wales
		1971—72	Wales

6. Rugby League

Challenge Cup Winners (since 1946)

1946—7	Bradford Northern	1959—60	Wakefield Trinity
1947—8	Wigan	1960—1	St. Helens
1948—9	Bradford Northern	1961—2	Wakefield Trinity
1949—50	Warrington	1962—3	Wakefield Trinity
1950—1	Wigan	1963—4	Widnes
1951—2	Workington Town	1964—5	Wigan
1952—3	Huddersfield	1965—6	St. Helens
1953—4	Warrington	1966—7	Featherstone Rovers
1954—5	Barrow	1967—8	Leeds
1955—6	St. Helens	1968—9	Castleford
1956—7	Leeds	1969—70	Castleford
1957—8	Wigan	1970—71	Leigh
1958—9	Wigan	1971—72	Leeds

Golf

Golf was begun in Scotland about five hundred years ago and shares with Association Football the distinction of being a truly international game, for there are golf courses today in almost every country in the world.

British Open Championship Winners (since 1948)

1948	T. H. Cotton (Great Britain)	1961	A. Palmer (U.S.A.)
1949	A. D. Locke (South Africa)	1962	A. Palmer
1950	A. D. Locke	1963	R. J. Charles (New Zealand)
1951	M. Faulkner (unattached)	1964	A. Lema (U.S.A.)
1952	A. D. Locke	1965	P. W. Thomson
1953	B. Hogan (U.S.A.)	1966	J. W. Nicklaus (U.S.A.)
1954	P. W. Thomson (Australia)	1967	R. de Vicenzo (Argentina)
1955	P. W. Thomson	1968	G. J. Player South Africa
1956	P. W. Thomson		
1957	A. D. Locke	1969	A. Jacklin (Great Britain)
1958	P. W. Thomson	1970	J. Nicklaus (U.S.A.)
1959	G. J. Player (South Africa)	1971	L. Trevino (Mexico)
1960	K. Nagle (Australia)	1972	L. Trevino (Mexico)

Ryder Cup Competition (Professional) (since 1947)

1947 U.S.A. 11 matches—Great Britain 1 match
1949 U.S.A. 7 matches—Great Britain 5 matches
1951 U.S.A. 9½ matches—Great Britain 2½ matches
1953 U. S.A. 6½ matches—Great Britain 5½ matches
1955 U.S.A. 8 matches—Great Britain 4 matches
1957 Great Britain 7½ matches—U.S.A. 4½ matches
1959 U.S.A. 8½ matches—Great Britain 3½ matches
1961 U.S.A. 13 matches—Great Britain 8 matches
1963 U.S.A. 20 matches—Great Britain 6 matches (6 halved)
1965 U.S.A. 18 matches—Great Britain 11 matches (3 halved)
1967 U.S.A. 21 matches—Great Britain 6 matches (5 halved)
1969 Drawn. Each team won 13 matches (6 halved)

1971 U.S.A. 16 matches—Great Britain 11 (5 halved)

Walker Cup Competition (Amateur) (since 1947)

1947 U.S.A. 8 matches—Great Britain 4 matches
1949 U. S.A. 10 matches—Great Britain 2 matches
1951 U.S.A. 6 matches—Great Britain 3 matches
(3 matches halved)
1953 U.S.A. 9 matches—Great Britain 3 matches
1955 U.S.A. 10 matches—Great Britain 2 matches
1957 U.S.A. $8\frac{1}{2}$ matches—Great Britain $3\frac{1}{2}$ matches
1959 U.S.A. 9 matches—Great Britain 3 matches
1961 U.S.A. 11 matches—Great Britain 1 match
1963 U.S.A. 12 matches—Great Britain 8 matches
1965 11 matches each, with 2 halved
1967 U.S.A. 13 matches—Great Britain 7 matches (4 halved)
1969 U.S.A. 10 matches—Great Britain 8 matches (6 halved)
1971 Great Britain 12 matches—U.S.A. 10 matches (2 halved)

Lawn Tennis

This is a modern game born of one much older. Real, or Royal, Tennis was played centuries ago and is still played to a limited extent today, but it is an expensive game.

Wimbledon Champions (Men's Singles)

1879—80	J. T. Hartley	1896	H. S. Mahony
1881—6	W. Renshaw	1897—1900	R. E. Doherty
1887	H. F. Lawford	1901	A. W. Gore
1888	E. Renshaw	1902—6	H. L. Doherty
1889	W. Renshaw	1907	N. E. Brookes
1890	W. J. Hamilton	1908—9	A. W. Gore
1891—2	W. Baddeley	1910—13	A. F. Wilding
1893—4	J. Pim	1914	N. E. Brookes
1895	W. Baddeley	1915—18	*No competition*

1919	G. L. Patterson	1950	J. E. Patty
1920—1	W. L. Tilden	1951	R. Savitt
1922	G. L. Patterson	1952	F. A. Sedgman
1923	W. M. Johnston	1953	E. V. Seixas
1924	J. Borotra	1954	J. Drobný
1925	R. Lacoste	1955	M. A. Trabert
1926	J. Borotra	1956—7	L. A. Hoad
1927	H. Cochet	1958	A. J. Cooper
1928	R. Lacoste	1959	A. Olmedo
1929	H. Cochet	1960	N. A. Fraser
1930	W. T. Tilden	1961	R. Laver
1931	S. B. Wood	1962	R. Laver
1932	H. E. Vines, Jr.	1963	C. R. McKinley
1933	J. H. Crawford	1964	R. Emerson
1934—6	F. J. Perry	1965	R. Emerson
1937—8	J. D. Budge	1966	M. Santana
1939	R. L. Riggs	1967	J. S. D. Newcombe
1940—5	*No competition*	1968	R. Laver
1946	Y. Petra	1969	R. Laver
1947	J. A. Kramer	1970	J. D. Newcombe
1948	R. Falkenburg	1971	J. D. Newcombe
1949	F. Schroeder, Jr.	1972	S. Smith

Davis Cup (International Lawn Tennis Championship)

1947	U.S.A.	4,	Australia	1
1948	U.S.A.	5,	Australia	0
1949	U.S.A.	4,	Australia	1
1950	Australia	4,	U.S.A.	1
1951	Australia	3,	U.S.A.	2
1952	Australia	4,	U.S.A.	1
1953	Australia	4,	U.S.A.	2
1954	U.S.A.	3,	Australia	2
1955	Australia	5,	U.S.A.	0
1956	Australia	5,	U.S.A.	0

162

1957 Australia	3,	U.S.A.	2
1958 U.S.A.	3,	Australia	2
1959 Australia	3,	U.S.A.	2
1960 Australia	4,	Italy	1
1961 Australia	5,	Italy	0
1962 Australia	5,	Mexico	0
1963 U.S.A.	3,	Australia	2
1964 Australia	3,	U.S.A.	2
1965 Australia	4,	Spain	1
1966 Australia	4,	India	1
1967 Australia	4,	Spain	1
1968 U.S.A.	4,	Australia	1
1969 U.S.A.	5,	Romania	0
1970 U.S.A.	5,	G.F.D.	0
1971 U.S.A.	3,	Rumania	2
1972 U.S.A.	3,	Rumania	2

Yachting

Probably the most famous yachting event is the series of races for the America's Cup, first competed for in 1851. America has won every contest. Results since 1920:

1920 *Resolute* beat *Shamrock IV*
1930 *Enterprise* beat *Shamrock V*
1934 *Rainbow* beat *Endeavour*
1937 *Ranger* beat *Endeavour II*
1958 *Columbia* beat *Sceptre*
1962 *Weatherly* beat *Gretel*
1964 *Constellation* beat *Sovereign*
1967 *Intrepid* beat *Dame Pattie*
1970 *Intrepid* beat *Dame Pattie*

Cricket

Cricket became widespread in England in the seventeenth and eighteenth centuries, then became popular abroad as English settlers went to Australia, New Zealand, South

163

Africa, India, Pakistan and the West Indies, all of which today take part in the Test Match series. Other countries where cricket is played are Holland, the United States, Canada, South America and most British Colonies, though in none of these does the standard approach what is recognised as 'first class'—the standard of the main national competitions in the Test-playing countries.

The first major overseas tour by an English team was a visit to Australia in 1861—2. It was in Melbourne, in 1877, that Australia won the first of all Test Matches.

Records in Cricket

Some of the most interesting cricket records are the following:

Highest score in first-class cricket—499 not out (Hanif Mohammed, in Pakistan, 1959)

Highest score in Test cricket—365 not out (G. Sobers, West Indies, against Pakistan, in Kingston, 1958)

Highest known score in School cricket-628 not out (A.E. Collins, in a match at Clifton College, Bristol, 1899)

Greatest number of runs in first-class cricket—61,237 between 1905 and 1934 (Sir J. B. Hobbs)

Most runs scored off a six-ball over—36 (G. Sobers of Nottinghamshire, off M. Nash of Glamorgan, at Swansea, 1968)

Highest batting partnership—577 (V. S. Hazare and Gul Mahomed, in Indian cricket, 1947)

Highest score in a season—3,816 (D.C.S. Compton, in 1947, with an average of 90.85)

Greatest number of wickets by a bowler in one match—19 (J.C. Laker, for England against Australia, at Old Trafford, 1956, for 90 runs)

Greatest number of wickets in first-class cricket—4,187 between 1898 and 1930 (W. R. Rhodes)

Greatest total—1,107 (by Victoria against New South Wales, 1926)

Test Matches—England—Australia (The Ashes)

1876—7   Australia 1, England 1
1878—9   Australia 1
1880   England 1
1881—2   Australia 2, drawn 2
1882   Australia 1
1882—3   Australia 2, England 2
1884   England 1, drawn 2
1884—5   England 3, Australia 2
1886   England 3
1886—7   England 2
1887—8   England 1
1888   England 2, Australia 1
1890   England 2, abandoned 1
1891—2   Australia 2, England 1
1893   England 1, drawn 2
1894—5   England 3, Australia 2
1896   England 2, Australia 1
1897—8   Australia 4, England 1
1899   Australia 1, drawn 4
1901—2   Australia 4, England 1
1902   Australia 2, England 1, drawn 2
1903—4   England 3, Australia 2
1905   England 2, drawn 3
1907—8   Australia 4, England 1
1909   Australia 2, England 1, drawn 2
1911—12   England 4, Australia 1
1912   England 1, drawn 2
1920—1   Australia 5
1921   Australia 3, drawn 2
1924—5   Australia 4, England 1
1926   England 1, drawn 4
1928—9   England 4, Australia 1
1930   Australia 2, England 1, drawn 2
1932—3   England 4, Australia 1

1934	Australia 2, England 1, drawn 2
1936—7	Australia 3, England 2
1938	England 1, Australia 1, drawn 2, abandoned 1
1946—7	Australia 3, drawn 2
1948	Australia 4, drawn 1
1950—1	Australia 4, England 1
1953	England 1, drawn 4
1954—5	England 3, Australia 1, drawn 1
1956	England 2, Australia 1, drawn 2
1958—9	Australia 4, drawn 1
1961	Australia 3, England 1, drawn 1
1962—3	Australia 1, England 1, drawn 3
1964	Australia 1, drawn 4
1965—6	Australia 1, England 1, drawn 3
1968	Australia 1, England 1, drawn 3
1971	England 1, drawn 4
1972	England 2, Australia 2, drawn 1

English County Championship

1873	Gloucestershire and Nottinghamshire
1874	Derbyshire
1875	Nottinghamshire, Lancashire and Sussex
1876	Gloucestershire
1877	Gloucestershire
1878	Middlesex
1879	Nottinghamshire and Lancashire
1880	Nottinghamshire
1881	Lancashire
1882	Nottinghamshire and Lancashire
1883	Nottinghamshire
1884	Nottinghamshire
1885	Nottinghamshire
1886	Nottinghamshire
1887	Surrey
1888	Surrey
1889	Surrey, Lancashire and Nottinghamshire
1890	Surrey
1891	Surrey
1892	Surrey
1893	Yorkshire
1894	Surrey
1895	Surrey
1896	Yorkshire
1897	Lancashire
1898	Yorkshire
1899	Surrey
1900	Yorkshire
1901	Yorkshire

166

1902	Yorkshire	1937	Yorkshire
1903	Middlesex	1938	Yorkshire
1904	Lancashire	1939	Yorkshire
1905	Yorkshire	1946	Yorkshire
1906	Kent	1947	Middlesex
1907	Nottinghamshire	1948	Glamorgan
1908	Yorkshire	1949	Middlesex and Yorkshire
1909	Kent	1950	Lancashire and Surrey
1910	Kent	1951	Warwickshire
1911	Warwickshire	1952	Surrey
1912	Yorkshire	1953	Surrey
1913	Kent	1954	Surrey
1914	Surrey	1955	Surrey
1919	Yorkshire	1956	Surrey
1920	Middlesex	1957	Surrey
1921	Middlesex	1958	Surrey
1922	Yorkshire	1959	Yorkshire
1923	Yorkshire	1960	Yorkshire
1924	Yorkshire	1961	Hampshire
1925	Yorkshire	1962	Yorkshire
1926	Lancashire	1963	Yorkshire
1927	Lancashire	1964	Worcestershire
1928	Lancashire	1965	Worcestershire
1929	Nottinghamshire	1966	Yorkshire
1930	Lancashire	1967	Yorkshire
1931	Yorkshire	1968	Yorkshire
1932	Yorkshire	1969	Glamorgan
1933	Yorkshire	1970	Kent
1935	Yorkshire	1971	Surrey
1936	Derbyshire	1972	Warwickshire

Rowing

There is no official world championship, but the events at Henley Royal Regatta in Britain are generally recognised as indicating the champions. The two events which attract most interest are the Grand Challenge Cup and the Diamond Challenge Sculls.

Grand Challenge Cup (for Eights) (since 1949)

Year	Winner	Year	Winner
1949	Leander Club	1963	London Univ.
1950	Harvard Univ. (U.S.A.)	1964	Club Zjalghivis Viljnius (U.S.S.R.)
1951	Lady Margaret B. C. Cambridge	1965	Ratzerburger Ruderclub (W. Germany)
1952	Leander Club	1966	T.S.C. Berlin
1953	Leander Club	1967	S.C. Wissenschaft (E. Germany)
1954	Krylia Sovetov Club (U.S.S.R.)	1968	London Univ.
1955	Univ. of Pennsylvania (U.S.A.)	1969	S. C. Einheit Dresden (E. Germany)
1956	French Army	1970	A.S.K. Vorwarts Rostock (E. Germany)
1957	Cornell Univ. (U.S.A.)	1971	Tideway Scullers (Britain)
1958	Trud Club (U.S.S.R.)	1972	W.M.E. Moscow (U.S.S.R.)
1959	Harvard Univ. (U.S.A.)		
1960	Molesey R.C.		
1961	U.S.S.R. Navy		
1962	Central Sport Club (U.S.S.R.)		

Diamond Challenge Sculls (for Single Oarsmen)

Year	Winner	Time
1950	A. D. Rowe (Leander Club)	9 m. 11 s.
1951	T. A. Fox (Pembroke Coll. Camb.)	8 m. 59 s.
1952	M. T. Wood (Australia)	8 m. 12 s.
1953	T. A. Fox (London R. C.)	8 m. 12 s.
1954	P. Vlasic (Yugoslavia)	8 m. 42 s.
1955	T. Kocerka (Poland)	8 m. 33 s.
1956	T. Kocerka (Poland)	8 m. 37 s.
1957	S. A. Mackenzie (Australia)	8 m. 25 s.
1958	S. A. Mackenzie (Australia)	8 m. 6 s.
1959	S. A. Mackenzie (Australia)	8 m. 29 s.
1960	S. A. Mackenzie (Australia)	8 m. 3 s.
1961	S. A. Mackenzie (Australia)	8 m. 34 s.

1962	S. A. Mackenzie (Australia)	8 m. 38 s.
1963	G. Kuttmann (Switzerland)	8 m. 9 s.
1964	S. Cromwell (U.S.A.)	8 m. 6 s.
1965	D. M. Spero (U.S.A.)	7 m. 42 s.
1966	A. Hill (Germany)	8 m. 15 s.
1967	M. Studach (Switzerland)	8 m. 27 s.
1968	H. E. A. Wardell—Yerburgh (Eton Vikings)	10 m. 25 s.
1969	H. J. Bohmer (West Germany)	8 m. 6 s.
1970	J. Meissner (W. Germany)	8 m. 18 s.
1971	A. Demeddi (Argentine)	8 m. 8 s.
1972	A. Timoschinin	8 m. 10 s.

Oxford and Cambridge Boat Race (Putney to Mortlake)

1829	Oxford	1864	Oxford
1836	Cambridge	1865	Oxford
1839	Cambridge	1866	Oxford
1840	Cambridge	1867	Oxford
1841	Cambridge	1868	Oxford
1842	Oxford	1869	Oxford
1845	Cambridge	1870	Cambridge
1846	Cambridge	1871	Cambridge
1849	Cambridge	1872	Cambridge
1849	Oxford	1873	Cambridge
1852	Oxford	1874	Cambridge
1854	Oxford	1875	Oxford
1856	Cambridge	1876	Cambridge
1857	Oxford	1877	Drawn
1858	Cambridge	1878	Oxford
1859	Oxford	1879	Cambridge
1860	Cambridge	1880	Oxford
1861	Oxford	1881	Oxford
1862	Oxford	1882	Oxford
1863	Oxford	1883	Oxford

1884	Cambridge	1924	Cambridge
1885	Oxford	1925	Cambridge
1886	Cambridge	1926	Cambridge
1887	Cambridge	1927	Cambridge
1888	Cambridge	1928	Cambridge
1889	Cambridge	1929	Cambridge
1890	Oxford	1930	Cambridge
1891	Oxford	1931	Cambridge
1892	Oxford	1932	Cambridge
1893	Oxford	1933	Cambridge
1894	Oxford	1934	Cambridge
1895	Oxford	1935	Cambridge
1896	Oxford	1936	Cambridge
1897	Oxford	1937	Oxford
1898	Oxford	1938	Oxford
1899	Cambridge	1939	Cambridge
1900	Cambridge	1940—45	*No contest*
1901	Oxford	1946	Oxford
1902	Cambridge	1947	Cambridge
1903	Cambridge	1948	Cambridge
1904	Cambridge	1949	Cambridge
1905	Oxford	1950	Cambridge
1906	Cambridge	1951	Cambridge
1907	Cambridge	1952	Oxford
1908	Cambridge	1953	Cambridge
1909	Oxford	1954	Oxford
1910	Oxford	1955	Cambridge
1911	Oxford	1956	Cambridge
1912	Oxford	1957	Cambridge
1913	Oxford	1958	Cambridge
1914	Cambridge	1959	Oxford
1915—19	*No contest*	1960	Oxford
1920	Cambridge	1961	Cambridge
1921	Cambridge	1962	Cambridge
1922	Cambridge	1963	Oxford
1923	Oxford	1964	Cambridge

1965	Oxford	1969	Cambridge
1966	Oxford	1970	Cambridge
1967	Oxford	1971	Cambridge
1968	Cambridge	1972	Cambridge

Cross Country

International Championship (since 1946)

1946 France	1954 England	1962 England
1947 France	1955 England	1963 Belgium
1948 Belgium	1956 France	1964 England
1949 France	1957 Belgium	1965 England
1950 France	1958 England	1966 England
1951 England	1959 England	1967 England
1952 France	1960 England	1968 England
1953 England	1961 Belgium	1969 England
		1970—72
		England

Swimming

Standards of swimming have improved very rapidly during the last hundred years as new stokes have been discovered. The 'marathon' in swimming is the Channel swim. This was first achieved in 1874 by Captain M. Webb (Britain), in 21 hours and 45 minutes; in 1950, a time of 10 hours and 50 minutes by Hassan Abdel Rehim (Egypt) was recorded.

World Records (Free-style)

Distance	Holder ·	Nation	Time
100 m.	M. Spitz	U.S.A.	51.5 s
200 m.	M. Spitz	U.S.A.	1 min. 53.5 s
400 m.	K. Krumpholz	U.S.A.	4 min. 00.1 s
1,500 m.	R. DeMont	U.S.A.	15 min. 52.9 s

Walking

World Records

Distance	Holder	Nation	Time	Year
20,000 m	P. Frenkel	East Germany	1 hr 25 min 50.0 s	1970
30,000 m	A. Yegorov	U.S.S.R.	2 hr 17 min 16.8 s	1959
30,000 m	C. Hohne	Germany	2 hr 15 min 16.0 s	1971
20 miles	A. Vedyakov	U.S.S.R.	2 hr 31 min 33.0 s	1958
30 miles	C. Hohne	Germany	4 hr 00 min 06.4 s	1969
30 miles	P. Selzer	East Germany	3 hr 56 min 12.6 s	1971
50,000 m	C. Hohne	Germany	4 hr 08 min 05.0 s	1969
50,000 m	P. Selzer	East Germany	4 hr 04 min 19.8 s	1971
26,658 m	P. Frenkel	East Germany	2 hours	1971

Ice-Skating

World Speed Champions (Men) (since 1947)

1947 L. Parkkinen (Finland)
1948 O. Lundberg (Norway)
1949 K. Pajor (Hungary)
1950 H. Andersen (Norway)
1951 H. Andersen
1952 H. Andersen
1953 O. Goncharenko (U.S.S.R.)
1954 B. Schilkov (U.S.S.R.)
1955 S. Ericsson (Sweden)
1956 O. Goncharenko
1957 K. Johanessen (Norway)
1958 O. Goncharenko
1959 J. Jaervinen (Finland)
1960 B. Stein (U.S.S.R.)
1961 H. van der Grift (Holland)
1962 V. Kosichkin (U.S.S.R.)
1963 J. Nilsson (Sweden)
1964 K. Johanessen (Norway)
1965 P. Moe (Norway)
1966 K. Verkerk (Holland)
1967 K. Verkerk (Holland)
1968 F. Maier (Norway)
1969 D. Fornaes (Norway)
1970 A. Schenk (Netherlands)
1971 A. Schenk (Netherlands)
1972 A. Schenk (Netherlands)

Table Tennis

This table-top version of Lawn Tennis is played in almost every country of the world, and in Asia and Central Europe it has become one of the major sports.

Organised table tennis came in 1927, with the formation of the English Table Tennis Association.

World Championships

Men's Singles

1950—51	J. Leach (England)
1951—52	H. Satoh (Japan)
1952—53	F. Sido (Hungary)
1953—54	I. Ogimura (Japan)
1954—55	T. Tanaka (Japan)
1955—56	I. Ogimura (Japan)
1956—57	T. Tanaka (Japan)
1957—58	*No Championship*
1958—59	Jung Kuo-Tuan (China)
1959—60	*No Championship*
1960—61	Chuang Tse-tung (China)
1961—62	*No Championship*
1962—63	Chuang Tse-tung (China)
1963—64	*No Championship*
1964—65	Chuang Tse-Tung (China)
1965—66	*No Championship*
1966—67	N. Hasegawa (Japan)
1967—68	*No Championship*
1968—69	F. Itoh (Japan)
1969—70	*No Championship*
1970—71	S. Bengtsson (Sweden)

Swaythling Cup (Men's Championship)

1950—51	Czechoslovakia
1951—52	Hungary

1952—53	England
1953—54	Japan
1954—55	Japan
1955—56	Japan
1956—57	Japan
1957—58	*No Championship*
1958—59	Japan
1959—60	*No Championship*
1960—61	China
1961—62	*No Championship*
1962—63	China
1963—64	*No Championship*
1964—65	China
1965—66	*No Championship*
1966—67	Japan
1967—68	*No Championship*
1968—69	Japan
1969—70	*No Championship*
1970—71	China

Gallery of Sportsmen

BANNISTER, Roger. While a medical student at Oxford, Bannister ran his way into the history books when he won a mile race on the University's Iffley Road track in the time of 3 minutes, 59.4 seconds, on June 6, 1954. It was the first time that the magic four minutes had been beaten. Shrewd training had brought Bannister this success, and though John Landy broke the record shortly afterwards, Bannister showed that his run was no fluke by soundly beating Landy in the 1958 Empire Games mile.

BRADMAN, Sir Donald. Born in New South Wales in 1908, Bradman became almost a run-making machine in cricket. He only falls short of comparison with Sir Jack Hobbs in his inability to really master difficult wickets. Bradman scored a century in his first first-class appearance.

He played in Australian cricket from 1927 to 1949. His career figures were 28,067 runs in 338 innings, averaging 95.14. He got 117 centuries, reached 200 37 times, and 300 six times. His top score of 452 not out stood as a world record for 29 years. He played in 52 test matches, 24 of them as captain. His test average was 99.94 including 29 centuries. Since his retirement, Sir Donald has worked as a journalist and test selector.

COMPTON, Denis. Compton was probably the most successful cricketer and footballer Britain has produced. As a right-hand bat and slow left-arm bowler, he played his first game for Middlesex in 1936, gaining his country cap the same year. Despite knee trouble towards the end of his career, Compton became a dashing bat and played in more than 70 Test matches. He scored 3,000 runs in one season and 2,000 on five occasions. His soccer career was with Arsenal, with whom he gained a League Championship medal (1947—48) and Cup Winner's medal (1949—50).

COTTON, Henry. Cheshire-born, Cotton became a professional golfer at 17. His concentration and ability to bring out the best at the right time made him one of the greatest golfers in this country in the 1930s. In 1934, he won the British Open, ending a ten-year monopoly of the title by Americans. In 1937 and 1938, he won it again against the best the Americans could produce. He still holds many British records (including his 65 in the 1934 Open Championship) and even at the age of 49, in 1956, he was able to finish 17th in the U.S. Open and 6th in the British Open.

DAVIS, Joe. It is unlikely that any man has so dominated a sport, and for so long, as Joe Davis has with snooker. He became World Professional Snooker Champion in 1927 and United Kingdom Billiard Champion in 1928. He held these two titles for every year up to 1946. Davis holds the world record professional snooker break of 147 and has made more than 600 breaks of over 100. His highest billiard break is 2,501. Davis summed up his career when he was asked if he had any ambitions left in the game. "All my ambitions have been realised," he said.

DEAN, Dixie. Born in Birkenhead, Dixie Dean grew to become the finest header of the ball soccer has ever seen, scoring nearly half his goals with it. Though he started his football career with Tranmere, he did not find fame till he moved to Everton. There, he created the record for most goals in a season (60 in 1927—28). From 1931 to 1933 he scored over 100 goals for Everton, helping them in their hat-trick of 2nd Division Championship, 1st Division Championship and the Cup in successive seasons. Dean gained 16 International caps between 1927 and 1933.

DEMPSEY, Jack. Born William Harrison, he took the name Jack Dempsey for his ring career but he was known more often than not as the Manassa Mauler. This title was well earned, for Dempsey had a rough early career in the ring, often going hungry if he lost a bout. It was because of this that he developed his killer instinct in the ring. By 1919, his rough style had brought him to challenge Jess Willard for the World Heavyweight Championship. Though conceding 4 stone to the giant Willard, he won in 3 rounds. It was not until 1926 that his title was taken from him by Gene Tunney. Though Dempsey lost his second fight as well to Tunney, it featured the famous 'long count' which favoured Tunney. A favourite with the crowds, Dempsey turned to refereeing when his fighting days were over.

DI STEFANO, Alfredo. Real Madrid, the Spanish football team, reached a state of supremacy in European football during the early 1950s that is unlikely to be surpassed. They won the European Cup for the first five years it existed. No player helped the team more to reach this standard than Alfredo di Stefano (he scored in all five finals from the centre forward position, a superb goal-scorer with brilliant ball control). Born in the Argentine, Di Stefano had a short spell in Colombia before coming to Spain to play for Barcelona and finally settling with Real Madrid.

ELLIOTT, Herb. By 1957, with the world record for the mile held at 3 mins., 57.2 secs. by Derek Ibbotson, it was thought that any further improvement on that would only be in tenths of a second. However, on August 6, 1958, Herb Elliot ran the mile in 3 mins., 54.5 secs., knocking nearly three seconds off the record. It was the greatest improvement on the mile record since the turn of the century, yet one to be expected from this Australian. Under the coaching of Percy Cerrutty, Elliott was producing exceptional times even as a youngster. He capped his career by winning the 1,500 metres in world record time at the 1960 Olympic Games, then retired in 1962 to give more time to his family and to his studies at Cambridge University.

EVANS, Godfrey. One of the finest wicket keepers cricket has seen, Evans started his career as a batsman, but tried his skill behind the stumps during the war. Though he first played for Kent in 1939, the war interfered with his career and it was not until 1946 that he gained his county cap. His first test was in 1946 and this was followed with over 90 test matches. In 1952 he got 100 test wickets and 1,000 test runs. The 1954 season saw him create his world record of 131 test wickets.

FANGIO, Juan Manuel. This Argentine racing driver was world champion in 1951, '54, '55, '56, and '57. For the whole decade he was the finest driver and, if he failed to win, it was more often the fault of the machine than the man. It is said that Stirling Moss styled himself on the relaxed Fangio. As an example of his consistency, Fangio's record for the 1957 season was:—1st in the Monaco, Argentine, French and German Grands Prix, and 2nd in the Pescara and Italian Grands Prix.

FRY, C. B. Charles Burgess Fry was undoubtedly sport's finest all-rounder. Born in Croydon in 1872, he died in Hampstead in 1956, aged 84. Though principally known for his achievements at cricket, he played for England at soccer, for Southampton in the 1902 F.A. Cup Final, gained an athletic blue for Oxford and for 21 years held the world long jump record of 23'5". Fry only just failed to gain a rugby blue and there were other minor sports at which he excelled. His county cricket career spanned thirty years; he played in 26 test matches and on one occasion captained England. His academic career was just as brilliant as his remarkable sporting achievements.

GALLACHER, Hughie. Though only 5'5" tall, Gallacher made up for this deficiency with amazing footwork which made him the finest centre forward in the country around the 1930s. Only a short temper handicapped his game. Starting his soccer with Airdrie, he moved in 1925 to Newcastle and then on to Chelsea, but not before he had become a Tyneside idol. In his career in League soccer, he scored 386 goals and gained 19 Scottish caps.

GONZALES, Pancho. In 1949, Pancho Gonzales won the Wimbledon and French doubles titles with Frank Parker. This was as high as this American ever got in the amateur game, for in October of that year he turned professional. With Jack Kramer's players, he toured the world in professional tournaments. Within a couple of years he had become their supreme champion, an exceptional athlete and a player with virtually no flaws. No matter who Kramer signed professionally, none could match the speed or power of Gonzales' game.

GRACE, W. G. The first name one thinks of in cricket history, and well one might, for Grace's career figures of 54,896 runs, 2,876 wickets and 871 catches will probably never be equalled. Born in Bristol in 1848, Grace played for West Gloucestershire at the age of nine and made his first-class debut at seventeen. By the time he reached his last game in 1908, he had created more cricket records than any other player. He played in 22 tests, being captain 13 times. It is thought that in all the games he played in, he scored 80,000 runs and took 7,000 wickets. He died in 1915.

HARRIS, Reg. Harris was Britain's greatest world class racing cyclist during the years following World War II. He became World Professional Sprint Champion in 1949, and held it for the two following years, then regained it in 1954. In 1951 he won the Trophie Gentil, the highest honour in international cycling, and despite the lack of interest in the sport in Britain (compared with the continental countries), he became Sportsman of the Year in 1949 and 1951. His Grand Prix victories include Copenhagen and Amsterdam (four times each) and Paris (twice).

HOBBS, Sir John ('Jack'). Recognised as possibly the finest batsman ever. Born at Cambridge in 1882, he played a few games for that county, then offered his services to Essex, who turned him down. Surrey accepted him, and from 1905 to 1934 he scored 61,237 runs (averaging 50.65) including 197 centuries. His test career lasted from 1907 to 1930, and included 5,410 runs at an average of 56.94. Besides topping the averages for many seasons, in 1920 he topped both the batting and bowling averages. This great Knight of Cricket died in 1963.

JAMES, Alex. A favourite with the crowds, Alex James of the familiar baggy pants (said to hide his leg movements from his opponents) was known as a top goal-scorer with Preston North End. But it was not until 1929, when he was transferred to Arsenal, that Herbert Chapman converted him into a great goal-maker. James became the linkman between defence and attack, sending long, shrewd passes to his foraging forwards. James was an extremely clever reader of the game and he played a big part in Arsenal's golden era of the 1930s, and, indeed, in the change of English soccer tactics in general.

JONES, Bobby. On statistics alone, the American Bobby Jones was the greatest golfer of them all; he won 13 major championships between 1923 and 1930. These included 4. U.S. Open, 3 British Open, 5 U.S. Amateur and 1 British Amateur. His superb swing is still modelled by top players today. In 1930 he achieved the Grand Slam of the four leading major golf championships.

LARWOOD, Harold. Born in Nottinghamshire in 1904, Larwood became a great fast bowler, yet his career was marred by controversies over his action and by a foot injury towards the end of his career. He played in 21 tests from 1926 to 1933 and was the main figure in the bodyline bowling controversy of that last year. In his career (lasting fourteen years) he took 1,427 wickets at an average of 17.51 runs. He now lives in Australia.

LOUIS, Joe. (Real name Joseph Barrow.) He was born in Alabama in 1914, became a professional boxer at 20 and won his first 27 fights. In 1936, Louis had become a sure prospect for the World Heavyweight Championship, but unaccountably lost to Max Schmeling. Two years later he won the title by defeating James Braddock. In the return with Schmeling, champion Louis took only 2 minutes 4 seconds to beat him. Louis remained undefeated champion until 1949, when he retired after 25 successful defences of his title. Only three challengers had stayed the distance against the mighty Louis. A come-back to the ring, to help pay tax debts, failed. Yet today he is still a rich man.

MATTHEWS, Sir Stan. Possibly the greatest name in soccer, Stan Matthews was born at Hanley, in the Potteries. He joined Stoke City as a professional at the age of 17, after being a prodigy in schoolboy international football. His famous body-swerve and ball control turned him into a living legend and he proved the biggest box office draw ever. At the age of 47 he was transferred to Blackpool, but returned to his original club of Stoke City in 1961—62. Matthews first played for England during the 1934—35 season at the age of 19. His last international appearance was in 1956—57. In all he made 84 international appearances. In 1957, he was voted Footballer of the Year, and in 1958 he got the C.B.E. for his services to sport. Returned to help his old club, Stoke City, in 1961, and was knighted in 1965.

NUVOLARI, Tazio. This Italian racing driver has been hailed as the greatest ever; he certainly was the finest of the pre-war period. He came from Mantua, but it was on the race tracks of the world that the crowds came to watch the maestro. His grand prix wins crowd the record books—undoubtedly his greatest win was in the 1935 German Grand Prix race when, with an outdated Alfa Romeo, he beat the powerful state-backed German racing teams. In 1938, Nuvolari transferred from Alfa Romeo, and he was one of the few drivers to master the rear-engined German Auto Union Grand Prix car.

OWENS, Jesse. This coloured American became the greatest sprinter of them all and dominated an Olympic Games more than any man has done since. An athlete of superb build and economy of movement, he had no equal over the short distances. By the time of the 1936 Olympic Games in Berlin, Owens held the world records for the 100 yards, 100 metres, 200 metres, 220 yards, 200 metres hurdles, 220 yards hurdles and the long jump. Hitler came to the Games to see German dominance. Instead, he saw the greatest one-man show of all time when Jesse Owens won the 100 metres, 200 metres, long jump and gained a fourth gold medal with the winning U.S. team in the 4×100 metres relay.

PERRY, Fred. Born in Stockport in 1909, Fred Perry first made his mark in the world of sport with table tennis, winning the Men's Doubles and Mixed Doubles titles in the English Open Championships. He then turned his exceptional powers of concentration and will-to-win to lawn tennis. He reached the last 16 at Wimbledon at his first appearance in 1928. It was a sign of things to come, for he won the Wimbledon title three years running, 1934, '35 and '36. He was voted the world's No. 1. in those same years. He won the American singles in 1933, '34 and '36, then turned professional in 1936. In 1962, he returned from coaching in America to help Great Britain in her bid to develop a winning Davis Cup team.

PUSKAS, Ferenc. Hungary's captain when they came to England in 1953, he led his national team to a 6—3 win. It was the first time a foreign team had beaten England in England. Puskas was a Hungarian Army officer who played as inside forward for his country. All the team relied on brilliant ball control to win. Puskas had this plus a left-foot shot that was one of the best in the world. Under his leadership, Hungary became the finest team in the world and might well have won the 1954 World Cup had it not been for an injury to Puskas in the Final when they were two goals up to Germany. When the Hungarian Revolution broke out in 1956, Puskas left his country and joined the famed Real Madrid. Alongside of Di Stefano, Puskas produced his previous best, despite his age.

RICHARDS, Sir Gordon. His record speaks for itself: Champion jockey 26 times, the first in 1925 and the last in 1953; and 4,870 winners. No jockey has matched that record and there was probably none so popular as the diminutive Sir Gordon. All his life the Derby had eluded him. Many thought that a Derby win was beyond him until 1953, when he eventually won on Pinza, to the delight of the whole racing world. When Sir Gordon finished riding, he became a successful trainer.

SULLIVAN, John L. Sullivan was the last of the great bare knuckle fighters and the most successful to convert to the gloves. Known as the Boston Strong Boy, his proud boast was that he could lick any man in the world. Born in 1858, it was not till 1882 that he caught up with the American heavyweight champion Paddy Ryan. Sullivan knocked him out in $10\frac{1}{2}$ minutes in a bare knuckle contest to become recognised generally as World Champion. He held this title until 1892 when he was knocked out in the 21st round in his fight with Jim Corbett at New Orleans.

WILDE, Jimmy. Weighing little over 7 stone, this Pontypridd flyweight started boxing in the old classic tradition. Over 700 boxing booth fights produced a superb fighting machine and a boxer with the hardest punch that had ever been seen at his weight. Wilde won the British title in 1916 by beating Joe Symonds. In the same year, the Americans sent over their world champion, Young Zulu Kid. Wilde K.O.'d him in 11 rounds to take the World Flyweight Championship—a title he held until 1923.

WRIGHT, Billy. Captain of Wolverhampton Wanderers for many years, Wright also became England's most successful and consistent captain. His 105 caps for England has never been equalled. Originally a right half, he was nearly rejected by Wolves at the age of 15. It was not until the 1954 World Cup that he was moved to the centre half position, where he was able to control the England team with even greater success in the following years. He retired from playing in 1959.

ZÁTOPEK, Emil. This Czech Army Officer won the 10,000 metres in the 1948 Olympic Games in London. It was not until he started producing world record times with apparent ease after this performance that the athletic world focused its attention on his training methods. They found that Zátopek was covering phenomenal distances each week in his torturous training schedules. It led to many of his contemporaries adopting this technique with success. Zátopek was the dominating runner in the 1952 Olympics, winning the 5,000 and 10,000 metres, and finally running away with the Marathon race.

PEOPLE AND LEISURE

Here are some of the dozens of spare-time activities which may appeal to you—ranging from camping to stamp collecting, from model-making to keeping tortoises.

Use of the Road

The open road is yours—on your bicycle or on foot—but your right to use it involves responsibilities on your part in return.

Cyclists, though they don't have to pass a driving test, must be fully aware of the Highway Code for their own safety as well as that of others. They are also obliged *by law* to have efficient brakes on *both* wheels, and a means of warning (either a bell or a horn). After dark they *must* have a headlamp, a red tail-lamp and a red reflector at the rear. Cyclists are also advised to wear light-coloured clothes at night—and this is a safety measure for those on foot as well, particularly in country districts where because of the absence of a pavement it is necessary to walk along the edge of the road. Whenever walking on the road, whether by day or by night, you should *face* the oncoming traffic.

Cyclists should give clear hand-signals before making left or right turns, by raising the appropriate arm shoulder-high. On slowing down or stopping, the correct signal is an up-and-down movement of the right arm.

What the Highway Code tells you can be roughly summarised as follows:

For Pedestrians

1. Where there is no footpath, walk *facing* oncoming traffic.
2. Before crossing the road, look right, look left, then look

right again. Cross at right-angles, use zebra crossings, central refuges or other pedestrian aids whenever possible, and take extra care if your view is limited or blocked in any way.

3. Before stepping on to a zebra crossing, allow approaching traffic ample time to stop. Remember that when a zebra crossing has a central refuge each half of the crossing must be treated separately.

4. At junctions, always watch for vehicles turning the corner.

5. If there is a police officer controlling traffic, be guided by his signals.

6. Do not get on or off any moving vehicle.

For Cyclists

1. When moving off, make the signal for a right turn before pulling out from the kerb.

2. Keep well to the left, except when overtaking or turning right.

3. Always, in riding at night, make sure you could pull up within the range of your lights. If dazzled by oncoming lights, slow down or stop.

4. Slow down before bends and sharp corners.

5. Give way to pedestrians on zebra crossings. They have the legal right of way. At crossings controlled by lights or police, give way to pedestrians already on the crossing when the signal to move is given.

6. When making a turn at a junction, remember that pedestrians who are crossing have the right of way.

7. Look out for pedestrians on country roads, and give them ample room, particularly at left-hand bends.

8. Go slow when passing animals, and give them plenty of room.

9. Do not overtake near corners, road junctions or pedestrian crossings, or when approaching the brow of a hill, a humpback bridge or a narrower section of road. Be extremely careful about overtaking at dusk or in fog.

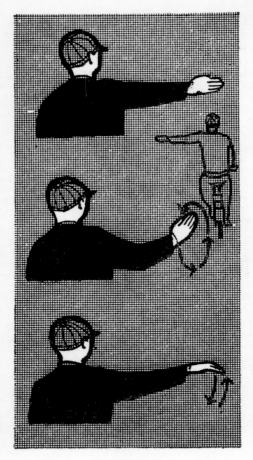

I am about
to turn right.

I am about
to turn left.
(for cyclists)

I am about
to turn left.
(for motorists)

I am about
to slow down
or stop.

186

10. Overtake on the right, except when the driver or rider in front has signalled that he intends to turn right.
11. Never cross a continuous white line along the middle of the road unless you can see a clear road ahead.
12. When approaching a road junction where there is a 'Slow' sign, slow down and be prepared to stop if necessary. At a 'Halt' sign you *must* stop at the major road, even if it is clear.
13. To turn right, signal in good time and take up a position just left of the middle of the road. For left turns keep over to the left, signal well in advance and avoid swinging out to the right.
14. When you draw up, pull in close to the near side of the road.
15. When riding, glance behind before you signal, move off, change course, overtake or turn.
16. Slow down, look both ways and listen carefully before going through a railway level crossing that has no gates. When there are unattended gates, open both gates before crossing, then close them after you. *Do not stop on the lines.* Never cross the lines when a warning signal is flashing or when the barriers have not lifted after the passing of a train—another train may be on the way.
17. If there is a track for cycles, use it.
18. *Never* ride more than two abreast, carry anything which could interfere with your control of your bicycle, hold on to another vehicle or cyclist, or ride close behind a moving vehicle.
19. It is against the law to stop a bicycle within the limits of a pedestrian crossing, except in circumstances beyond your control or to avoid an accident.
20. It is illegal to ride on a footpath, or to carry a passenger on a bicycle not built or adapted for more than one.
21. It is illegal to ride recklessly, to interrupt the free passage of another road user or to leave your cycle on the road in such a way that it could cause danger to others.

Here are some of the new road signs.

WARNING SIGNS

T junction | Series of bends | STOP sign ahead | GIVE WAY sign ahead | Slippery road | Low-flying aircraft

REGULATORY SIGNS

Police stop | Ahead only | No entry | Speed limit (max.) | Speed limit end | Laden weight limit

INFORMATORY SIGNS

Count-down markers (bar = 100 yards) to motorway or primary route exit | •Advance warning of no through road | Appropriate lanes at junction ahead

Country Code

1. Avoid dangers of fire. Be sure any cooking fires are extinguished before you move on.
2. Fasten all gates after use.
3. Keep dogs under control.
4. When crossing farm land keep to the path.
5. Do not damage fences, hedges or walls.
6. Leave no litter. You can be heavily fined for leaving rubbish behind.
7. Protect wild life, plants and trees.
9. Respect the countryside.

188

Map-making and Map-reading

Start by making a map of your own district. The first thing you must do is decide what scale it is going to be. The most common scale is one inch to a mile (that is, one inch of map represents one mile of actual ground, and this is the one you will find on official maps such as the Ordnance Survey sheets). But for maps that only cover a small area you may prefer a scale of two inches to the mile, which will provide room for more details.

When you have the streets drawn and named, put in the most important landmarks, such as the police station, hospital, post office and doctor's house, after which you can go on and put in your friend's houses, the shops you use most frequently, your school and so on, until in the end you have the map completely filled.

You can also trace out in different colours the shortest routes from your home to important places, with the time it takes written beside each place. In this way you can tell at a glance the quickest way to any given place and know before you start how long it will take to get there.

Once you've mapped your own district, why not go out exploring and make maps of your trips? Take a printed map with you at first (preferably an Ordnance Survey map, as these are by far the best), and learn to read it so that you can see how it is made. You will see that the map is covered with all sorts of lines and signs which are a picture of what the ground actually looks like. These may look rather confusing at first, but understanding them is really quite easy.

Contour Lines

Contour lines tell you the height and slope of the ground. They measure off each increase in height of fifty feet and indicate the shape of the hills. The figures give the height above sea level and, of course, the closer they are together,

189

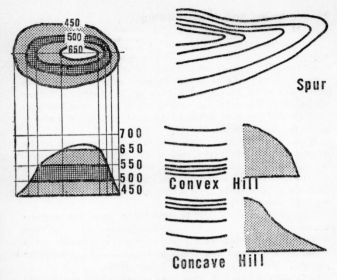

Spur

Convex Hill

Concave Hill

the steeper the slope is. If your map shows any coastline you will see similar lines for the depth of the sea.

Conventional Symbols

Certain symbols are used to show houses, churches, post offices, telegraph lines, viaducts, railway lines, trees—anything, in fact, that isn't just field. Most of these look like the things they represent, so they are easy to remember. Some of them are opposite, and you'll find others printed for you at the bottom of the Ordnance Survey maps.

Map References

If you're planning to meet a friend in the country it's obviously no good saying 'I'll meet you on the hill with trees

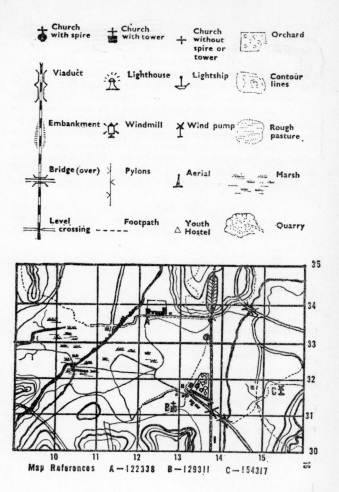

Church with spire	Church with tower	Church without spire or tower	Orchard
Viaduct	Lighthouse	Lightship	Contour lines
Embankment	Windmill	Wind pump	Rough pasture
Bridge (over)	Pylons	Aerial	Marsh
Level crossing	Footpath	Youth Hostel	Quarry

Map References A — 122338 B — 129311 C — 154317

on the top' because there might be half a dozen such hills. So, to make quite sure, you refer to your map.

If you look at the map you'll find that it is crossed by a number of horizontal and vertical lines. At the ends of each line is a two-figure number. Find the vertical line lower in number than your intended meeting-place, and note the figure down. Now your meeting-place will rarely be exactly on a line, so to make your map reference absolutely accurate imagine that the square is crossed by ten smaller lines. Decide which line your meeting place is on or nearest, and add its number to the two you've already got. If it is exactly between lines 12 and 13, your final figure will be 125. (If the place actually does fall on a line, put a nought after the grid number.)

Now do the same thing with your horizontal lines; then write the six figures out one after the other, placing the vertical reading first. You now have your final six-figure map reference.

Camping

Camping can be one of the most pleasant and rewarding of summer recreations, but a camping trip may be spoilt if some necessary item has been omitted from the gear, or, on the other hand, if you overload yourself by carrying things you don't need. The following checklist should prove helpful when you plan your camping trip.

Personal Equipment

Rucksack
Change of clothing
Change of underclothing
2 spare pairs of socks
Spare pair of shoes

192

Spare shoelaces
Pair of pyjamas
Handkerchiefs
Mackintosh
Warm pullover
Swimming costume
Towel (possibly 2)
Flannel
Soap
Toothbrush and paste
Brush and comb
Nail brush
Maps
Metal mirror
Compass
Pocket-knife
Water-bottle
Money

Equipment Shared among the Party

Tent
Tent-pegs
Cord
Small spade or trowel
Axe
Groundsheets
Sleeping bags (or blankets)
Spare blankets (if desired)
Inflatable mattresses and pillows
Torch, with spare batteries
Cooking stove
Fuel and matches
Stewing-pot, frying-pan and kettle
Plastic, aluminium or paper plates and mugs

193

Cutlery
Teacloth
Can and bottle opener
Food box (for perishable items)
Canvas bucket for washing
Small First Aid kit

Tents

If you are buying a tent for your trip, you will find illustrated below some of the many varieties from which to make a choice.

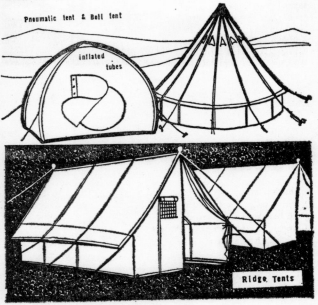

Pneumatic tent & Bell tent

inflated tubes

Ridge Tents

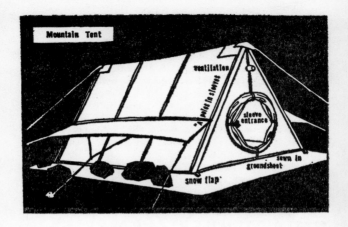

Youth Hostels

Hikers and cyclists wanting to use Youth Hostels can get full details of membership from their National Headquarters.

The rules vary slightly form country to country. In Britain you can join the Youth Hostels Association from the age of five onwards. Up to the age of nine you must be accompanied by a parent or legal guardian when using Youth Hostels, and up to twelve by any adult member. From twelve onwards members may use the Hostels without being accompanied.

Youth Hostels are for travellers on foot, by bicycle or by canoe; members touring by any power-assisted vehicle are barred. You may stay up to three consecutive nights at any one Hostel. Most Hostels provide meals at low charges; alternatively, cooking facilities are available. A list of National H. Q. addresses follows:—

England and Wales : Y.H.A., National Office, Trevelyan
House, St. Albans, Herts.
Scotland : S.Y.H.A., 7 Glebe Crescent, Stirling.
Northern Ireland : Y.H.A.N.I., 28 Bedford Street, Belfast.
Republic of Ireland : An Oige, 39 Mountjoy Square, Dublin.
Australia : A.Y.H.A., 492 George Street, Sydney, New South
Wales.
New Zealand : N.Z.Y.H.A., P.O. Box 436, Christchurch,
C 1.
South Africa : Y.H.A., P.O. Box 2,085, Johannesburg, S.A.
Canada : C.Y.H.A., 1,406 West Broadway, Vancouver 9,
British Columbia.
United States : American Youth Hostels Incorporated, 14
West 8th Street, New York, N.Y. 10011.

FIRST AID WHEN OUT AND ABOUT

When giving First Aid remember that unless you've had
training through the Red Cross or some similar organisation
you may do more harm by doing too much than too little.
Your attempts to treat serious burns or to straighten a fracture may make it more difficult for the doctor who later
has to cure the patient.

The *first* object of First Aid is to save life : that is, to prevent the casualty from dying before medical aid can be obtained. Therefore, look immediately for signs of asphyxia or
severe bleeding and, if necessary, stop bleeding and begin
artificial respiration. *Every second counts.*

The *second* object is to prevent any deterioration in the
condition of the casualty. This is achieved by attending
to the injuries which the casualty has sustained, and preven-
ting further injury.

Never attempt to give an unconscious person anything to drink.

ASPHYXIA

Asphyxia is a condition whereby air is prevented from entering the lungs of the body such as by Suffocation, Drowning, Gas, Choking and Strangulation.

Asphyxia can also occur in cases of electric shock.

If the casualty has stopped breathing do not lose an instant, act quickly and methodically.

1. Lay the casualty on his back and kneel beside his head.
2. Place one hand under his neck and the other hand on top of his head.
3. Lift the neck and tilt the head backwards as far as possible ; this may clear the airway and the casualty may begin to breathe. If he does not, immediately commence artifical respiration.

Artificial Respiration

Mouth to Mouth Method

1. Keep the head tilted backwards.
2. Move the hand from under the neck and place it on the patient's chin, with the thumb between the lower lip and the chin, the forefinger along the line of the jaw and the other fingers curled into the palm of the hand. This will avoid the hand pressing on the patient's neck. While doing this, open your mouth wide and breathe deeply.
3. Open your mouth wide, seal the casualty's mouth with your own and blow in.
4. Watch out of the corner of your eye, if possible, for the rise of the chest. Remove the thumb to allow a free passage of the expired air.

197

5. Repeat 3 and 4 twelve to fifteen times a minute, for a baby or small child the rate is twenty puffs a minute ceasing as the chest starts to rise. In no circumstances blow violently into a baby's lungs.

If no air appears to be getting into the lungs remove any obstruction that might be present in the mouth.

Revised Holger Nielsen Method

1. Lay casualty face down with head turned to one side, arms above his head with elbows bent so that the upper part of the cheek is resting on his hands.
2. Kneel at his head, placing one knee near casualty's head and one foot alongside his elbow (see Figs. 4 and 5).
3. Place your hands over casualty's shoulder blades, with thumbs touching in the mid-line and fingers spread out, the arms being kept straight (see Figs. 4 and 5).
4. Rock forward gently with arms straight and apply light pressure by weight of upper part of body only (see Fig. 1).
5. Rock back with arms straight, release pressure gradually, and slide your hands to elbows of casualty (see Fig. 2).
6. Raise and lift casualty's arms until tension is felt, (see Fig. 3), to cause inhalation.
7. Then lower casualty's arms down and place your hands on his back as in Fig. 1.
8. Repeat the above movement with rhythmic rocking at the rate of 12 times a minute, until breathing has been re-established.
9. If the arms are injured, place them by the sides of the body then do the complete procedure, but insert your hands under the casualty's shoulders and raise them for inhalation.

198

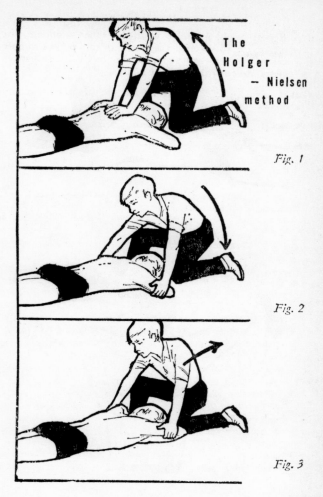

The
Holger
— Nielsen
method

Fig. 1

Fig. 2

Fig. 3

199

The Holger-Nielsen
method

Fig. 4

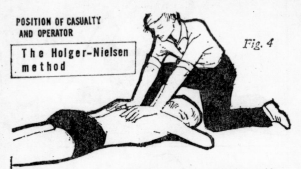

Place hands over casualty's shoulder – blades with thumbs touching
in the mid-line and arms straight

POSITION OF CASUALTY AND OPERATOR

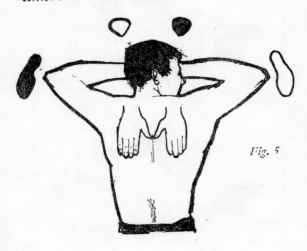

Fig. 5

200

Drowning

Do not lose an instant; act quickly and methodically.
1. Quickly clear mouth of any false teeth, weeds, or obvious obstruction.
2. Give mouth to mouth artifical respiration as described on page 197.
3. Maintain body heat of patient by placing rug or coat over and under him and continue artifical respiration until a doctor has pronounced the patient dead.
4. When consciousness returns, keep casualty lying down in recovery position and treat for shock.
5. Arrange for transport of casualty to hospital as soon as possible.

Electric Shock

Act promptly, taking care not to electrocute yourself.
1. Switch off current if possible or unplug cable.
2. If this is not possible stand on an insulating material (a dry folded mackintosh, or piece of wood) and pull casualty away by means of rope or walking stick, but not an umbrella which has metal ribs. If possible avoid contact with the casualty's armpits.
3. Apply Mouth to Mouth Resuscitation if breathing has stopped.
4. Transfer to hospital as soon as possible.

BLEEDING OR HAEMORRHAGE

External

Act immediately.
1. Lay casualty flat.
2. Raise bleeding part if there is no fracture.

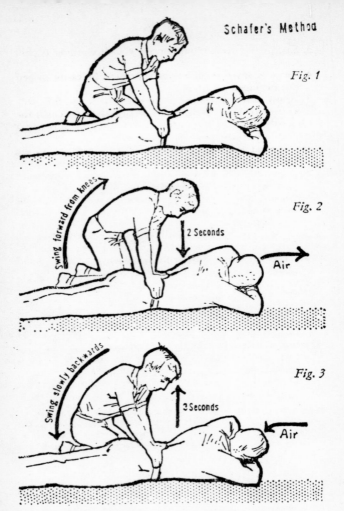

Schafer's Method

Fig. 1

Fig. 2

Swing forward from knees

2 Seconds

Air

Fig. 3

Swing slowly backwards

2 Seconds

Air

This is another method although no longer taught.

3. Expose the wound, but remove as little clothing as possible.
4. Remove any foreign bodies which can be easily picked out or wiped off.
5. Apply direct pressure to bleeding area, as follows:-
   (a) If there is no foreign body or broken bone, cover the wound with a clean dressing and maintain in position by a firm bandage.
   (b) If there is a foreign body or broken bone, cover the wound with a dressing and pad around the wound so that general pressure can be applied without pressure on the foreign body or broken bone.
6. If blood soaks through the bandage, apply more padding and bandage firmly on top of the previous bandage. (Do not remove the first dressing).
7. Do not disturb any blood clot.
8. If bleeding continues, apply firm finger pressure to appropriate arterial pressure point on the heartside of wound (see illustration on page 205).

SHOCK

1. Lay casualty on his back with head to one side and legs slightly raised, unless they are fractured.
2. Stop any bleeding.
3. Loosen clothing at neck and waist.
4. Maintain body heat of casualty by placing rug or coat around casualty. Do not give anything to drink or apply hot water bottles.
5. Handle as gently as possible and avoid any unnecessary movements.
6. See there is plenty of fresh air, and protect against any inclemency of weather.
7. Be cheerful and encouraging.
8. Get a doctor as soon as possible.

UNCONSCIOUSNESS

1. Examine the casualty to see that:
   (a) He is breathing — If not apply artificial respiration (see page 197).
   (b) He is not bleeding — If he is give appropriate treatment.
2. If the casualty is breathing normally, turn the head to one side and ensure a clear airway by tilting the head slightly backwards.
3. If for any reason the casualty appears to have noisy breathing, turn him into the Recovery Position.
4. Turn patient onto side with the leg and arm on the side on which he is lying stretched out behind him. The arm and leg which are in front of him should be bent so that the hip and elbow joints are at about a right angle. The head should be tilted slightly backwards.
5. Do not give patient anything to drink.

Fainting

1. If the casualty feels faint, sit him down and lower his head between the knees.
2. If unconscious, lay casualty down with head turned to one side, then feet. Do not leave unattended.
3. Loosen clothing at neck and waist.
4. Allow plenty of fresh air, but protect from cold.
5. When casualty regains consciousness gradually raise him and give sips of water, tea or coffee.

Burns and Scalds

Never handle a burned area and do not apply any lotions or ointment. The object of treatment of burns is to reduce the heat of the burn.

Application of Pressure
(Black circle indicates wound)

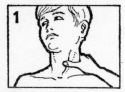

Carotid (finger pressure)

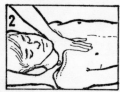

Subclavian (finger pressure)

Brachial (finger pressure
or constrictive bandage)

Femoral (finger pressure)

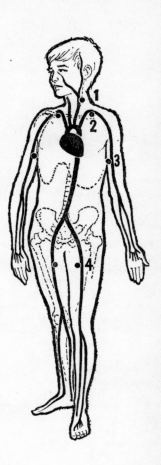

1. Place the burned area in cool clean water.
2. When pain has subsided apply a clean dry dressing.
3. Arrange for transport to hospital as soon as possible. The transport of a seriously burned patient to hospital should not be delayed.
4. Burn blisters should not be pricked.
5. Reassure the casualty, as this is most important to his recovery.

FRACTURES

Do not move casualty until injured part is immobilised, unless life is in immediate danger from surrounding environment i.e., falling buildings, fire etc.

Closed

1. Ensure casualty is in comfortable condition.
2. Keep warm, handle gently and generally guard against shock (see page 203).
3. Immobilise injured part by means of bandages and slings. The chest wall or the sound leg serve as good splints. In certain circumstances well padded splints may be required.
   (a) In the case of an arm, apply padding; bandage and support arm in a sling with the elbow bent and hand pointing to uninjured shoulder (illustrated on page 209).
   (b) If a leg, pad well between the knees and ankles; bandage the sound leg to the injured one.
4. Never try to set the bones.
5. Do not give food or drink, as anaesthetic may have to be given shortly.

Get a doctor or send to hospital quickly.

Open

Treat as for a simple fracture but, in addition:
1. Expose and cover the wound with a dry dressing.
2. Stop any bleeding (see pages 201—3).
3. Especially take care to counteract shock.
4. Do not try to push protruding bone back into place.

Dislocations

1. Support the limb in the most comfortable position. Use plenty of padding with bandages. Never attempt to reduce a dislocation.
2. Reassure the casualty which will help to control shock.
3. Guard against shock.
4. In cases of the lower jaw, remove any dentures if possible and support the jaw by a bandage tied over the top of the head.
5. Transfer patient to hospital.

Sprains and Strains

1. Immobilise injured part.
2. Apply cold compress where possible.
3. Do not remove shoe or boot, unless swelling of the foot is great.
4. Arrange for transport to hospital.
5. If there is any doubt as to the extent of the injury treat as a fracture.

Poisoning

Poisons fall ito two categories.
(a) Those poisons which burn.
(b) Those which do not burn.

Conscious Casualty

1. Ask the casualty exactly what happened.
2. (a) If there are no stains on the lips or mouth (indicating burning), make him vomit, by giving him an emetic (2 tablespoons of salt to a glass of water).
   (b) If there are stains DO NOT make him vomit, but dilute the poison by giving drinks of water, milk or barley water.
3. Transfer casualty to hospital at once without delay.

Unconscious Casualty

1. Ensure he is breathing freely; place him in the Recovery Position.
2. Should he not be breathing commence artificial respiration at once.
3. Transfer to hospital immediately.

Note: In all cases of poisoning any bottles or other containers found must be sent with the casualty to hospital.

SNAKE BITES

Generally speaking the only poisonous snake to be found in the wild state in Great Britain is the Adder, which is characteristically recognised by zig-zag lines on the snake's back.

1. It is very important to reassure the patient.
2. Lay the casualty down at absolute rest.
3. Tie a handkerchief or scarf very firmly round the limb just above the bite.
4. Wash the wound with soap and water.

5. Flush the area with clean cool water and cover with a clean dry dressing.
6. Splint the affected limb as for a fracture.
7. Transport the casualty to hospital as a stretcher case.

Examples

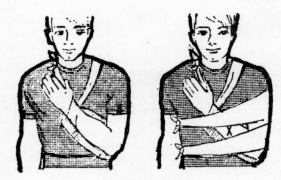

Fracture of arm

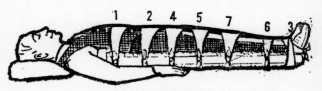

Fracture of thigh

Sketching and Painting

This is a hobby that can give anyone a great deal of enjoyment and satisfaction—even if he has always felt that he 'can't draw a straight line'. In fact, it is often those having the greatest doubts as to their ability who eventually produce the best results. Painting and drawing are wonderful ways of increasing your powers of observation, and they can provide a far more personal record of the things you see than the camera can ever hope to achieve.

For pencil sketching a beginner needs a range of soft and hard pencils, some sticks of soft charcoal, a block or book of cartridge paper, a soft india-rubber and a charcoal eraser. A small bottle of charcoal fixative, together with a blower, will be needed to 'fix' charcoal drawings.

Art classes at school may have taught the chief rule of perspective; briefly, it is that distant objects appear smaller. If you stand in the middle of a railway track and look along it, the two rails appear to draw closer together in the distance. This applies to all objects; the wall of a house, viewed at an angle, appears taller at the end nearest the point at which you are standing. Easy practice in perspective can be had by sketching open country with fields. Trees, hedges and fences will give you a challenge in perspective which will stand you in good stead when you tackle something more difficult.

Light and shade in pencil sketching are achieved by depth of pencil shading. There is no need to pay too much attention to the way in which this shading is applied, or to try to put in a great many details. The best way to begin is to look for the main masses of light and dark in front of you and to try to represent their shapes, as well as their sizes and tones in relation to one another. The more outstanding details that you see can be put in later. You should, however, bear in mind that a sketch of a scene is always a simplification of that scene.

Drawing in perspective

level view

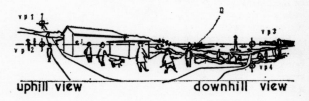

uphill view   downhill view

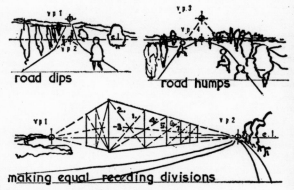

road dips   road humps

making equal receding divisions

V. P. = vanishing point
e.l. = eye level – of viewer
1,2,3,4,5,6,7. = order of construction lines

211

Should you wish to sketch in pen and ink—a more limiting medium for a beginner—you will need a harder-surfaced paper, a small range of nibs and a bottle of black India ink. You can also buy India ink in a variety of colours.

If you would like to try painting, you may choose to start with oil paints, water-colours, poster colours or even pastels. If you are beginning in oils, you will find prepared hardboard a satisfactory surface to use and inexpensive compared with canvas. It is best to equip yourself with large brushes, to use a good-sized surface, and to treat the subject matter broadly, looking for areas of colours and tones, and for their relations to one another. Try some exercises which will help you to see how one colour affects another; place patches of different colours, or of different shades of one colour, next to each other and study the effect. Some colours are heavier than others; some come forward while others seem to recede; asome combinations of colours are harmonious while some are discordant. All of these discoveries can be applied to your painting. Many other colour exercises can be found in the various books on painting which are in your public library.

You may find it useful to keep to a fairly small selection of colours at first. The following is a suggested basic palette for oil painting:

Cadmium Yellow
Cadmium Red
Alizarin Crimson
Monastral Blue
Ultramarine (blue)
Viridian (green)
Flake, Titanium or Zinc White
Ivory Black

Useful colours to add to this are Yellow Ochre, Light Red, Cobalt Blue and Terre Verte (earth green).

Film Sizes

Standard film sizes in general use for ordinary photography are the following:

Film Size (millimetres)	Pictures per Film	Size of Picture (inches)
35	36	$1 \times 1\frac{1}{2}$
127	16	$1\frac{1}{8} \times 1\frac{3}{4}$
127	12	$1\frac{3}{4} \times 1\frac{3}{4}$
127	8	$2\frac{1}{4} \times 1\frac{3}{4}$
120 and 620	16	$2\frac{1}{4} \times 1\frac{5}{9}$
120 and 620	12	$2\frac{1}{4} \times 2\frac{1}{4}$
120 and 620	8	$2\frac{1}{4} \times 3\frac{1}{4}$

Standard sizes of cine-film in general use are: 8, 9.5, 16 and 35 millimetres.

Film Scripting

The economical sizes of cine-film for amateurs are 8 and 9.5 millimetres. Silent film in both cases is exposed at 16 'frames' or pictures per second and projected at the same speed. Spoken commentaries for silent film should be based on a calculation of 3 words per second. Preparation of a running commentary is done by means of a table made on the following lines:

Scene	Second	Aggregate Seconds	Commentary
G/V Fishing village	3	3	Throughout Cornwall we found small fishing villages, most with only three
M/S Moored boats	2	5	or four boats.
C/U Elderly fisherman	3	8	Each boat is a family concern. This seventy-

M/CU Dad talks to him	2	0	year-old skipper told my father that he'd been at sea since he was only
C/U Hands Dad fish	6	16	eight—and gave Dad an odd-looking fish like an octopus!
T/S Deck of boat	2	18	They were unloading; most of the fish is sent up
L/V Wagons at dockside	4	22	to London by rail straight away.
C/U Curious fish	3	25	But we didn't send *our* odd fish! When the skipper wasn't looking, we
M/S Fish into hole; Mother holding her nose	4	29	dug a hole and buried it!

This family adventure, running half a minute approximately, takes just over a third of a 'roll' of 9.5 millimetre film, and a much smaller proportion in the case of 8 millimetre film.

Key to Standard Abbreviations used in Film Scripting

G/V = General view
L/V = Long view
M/S = Medium shot
T/S = Top shot
M/CU = Medium close-up
C/U = Close-up
B/V = Back view
PAN = Shot in which camera is swung sideways from one object to another or following a moving object
TILT = Shot in which camera is swung vertically from one object to another or following a moving object

Handicrafts

Not only is it far more fun and more satisfying to make things yourself, but it saves your pocket-money for the things which you *cannot* make. Here is the 'know-how' for some interesting 'make-it-yourself' projects, none of which needs special tools or equipment.

Making Model Railway Scenery

There's all the difference in the world between playing with toy trains and being a model railway enthusiast—and you can bridge that gap without digging deeply into your pocket. Scenery and buildings are expensive to buy; make them yourself at a fraction of the cost.

Scenery—hills, valleys, embankments, cliffs and so on—is best made from papier mâché. This doesn't involve fine modellers' papier mâché, which takes many hours to prepare. For tunnels, hills, etc., a rough, lumpy surface is realistic so lumpy papier mâché will do perfectly well. Fill a bucket with newspaper torn into small scraps, add a tablespoonful of size or a small square of carpenter's glue, then pour on boiling water and stir. Keep adding water and stirring until the mixture is like thick, lumpy porridge; let it cool enough to handle, and then use it to model your scenery. Painted in greens, brown and greys, it is far more realistic than any of the expensive scenery sold in modelling shops.

Railway buildings, houses, churches and factories are also easy to build, as long as you are satisfied with approximate scale. To reduce a building of your own local station to the standard '00' scale, count the number of bricks on an end wall, first vertically, then horizontally, and then allow seven bricks to the inch horizontally and twenty-two to the inch vertically.

Sturdy buildings can be made from card as long as the base is wooden. The method is very easy, and the sketch

215

below shows an example which is simple to adapt for other purposes. Once you understand how it's done, it requires only a little thought to apply it to any building of your own design.

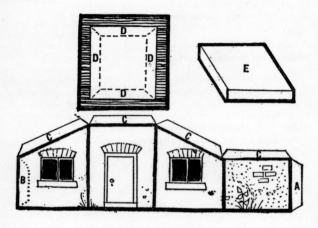

In this example of a plate-layer's hut, the roof could be painted grey or black and the walls covered with 'red-brick' paper—which costs only a few pence to buy. The chimney is a round wooden lollipop stick painted black. Before gluing A to B and C to D, fasten squares of cellophane on to the inside of each window. Finally, glue the completed building on to the base block E, which should fit snugly inside.

In this way stations, factories, houses and shops can be made cheaply and to designs which fit in with the layout of the track and the restrictions of space available.

Bookbinding

Whole works have been written on the *proper* way to set about binding books at home, but the methods described require a heavy press. This simple way of putting sturdy covers on paper-backed books needs nothing except scraps of material, cardboard, scissors, glue and common sense.

First find a piece of stiff material big enough to cover the book with an inch to spare all round. If no stiff material is handy, use a piece of an old sheet, well starched. Cut out three pieces of cardboard, the sizes of the front, back and spine of the book. Glue these to the material as in the diagram.

Now cut slots at A, bend the material down and glue on to the card. Next glue B to the front and back of the book. Fold down and glue the edges of the material, being careful to make neat, flat folds at the corners. Finally, paste white paper on the inside of each cover, to hide the folds of the material. If you want the title of the book on the spine, neat lettering on a strip of white paper glued into place will finish off a thoroughly professional-looking job.

Printing from Linocuts

You can make black-and-white pictures or full-colour illustrations for Christmas cards and other purposes by linocut printing. A piece of high-quality thick lino is needed. This can be bought ready cut from an art materials shop in sizes from 3×3 inches upwards, or can be trimmed from scraps after laying household lino. Thin lino isn't suitable, as the design for printing has to be cut into its surface. The lino should have a plain surface without any glossy design on it.

On the lino, draw the outlines of the picture which is to be made, remembering that the final result will be the exact reverse of your drawing. Avoid excessive detail; a picture drawn with a few bold strokes of the pencil is most likely to be successful. The outline should then be gone over with black India ink so that it will not be rubbed away by your hand while cutting the outlines.

You may already have a narrow 'V'-shaped chisel suitable for gouging out the unwanted areas of lino, but if not, one can be quite easily made from the broken rib of an old umbrella, fixed into a wooden handle and then ground to a sharp cutting edge. When all the areas which are not to be printed have been chiselled away, the picture is ready for inking.

This is done by means of a small roller and a piece of glass. The roller should be made of gelatine compound, and small ones can be obtained very cheaply at any art materials shop. So can small tubes of printing ink, and suitable paper.

Squeeze a small amount of printing ink on to the sheet of glass and work it to a thin, even surface with the roller which, of course, will then be similarly coated. Roll back and forth across the linocut; then place a sheet of printing paper on the linocut and press evenly and gently over the surface. This is best done with a circle of wood such as five-ply, of about four inches in diameter. This can easily be made with a fret-saw. The under side, which is to be used for pressing and rubbing, should have its edge smoothed off to prevent it from digging into the surface of the paper. Care should be taken that the lino does not slip while on the paper.

Cutting the block

Inking-up

The finished print.

Linocuts in more than one colour can be made in the same way. A block is made for each colour of the full picture, and the only extra problem is that of making sure that all blocks 'register' accurately—in other words, that the colours do not overlap where this is not intended. If the picture is first drawn on to tracing paper and the appropriate outlines are then transferred on to each block of lino, this problem should not arise.

Making a Kite

Some designs of kite are hard to build, but this one takes only an hour or so and needs no complicated tools. Start with three straight sticks, one thirty inches long, the other two twenty-five inches in length. Nail the centres of the two shorter pieces to the centre of the long piece, and open out the shorter pieces so that, if the long piece pointed to twelve and six on the clock, the shorter pieces would be set at two, four, eight and ten. Make a small hole in the ends of each stick, and run a piece of very fine wire from hole to hole, securing it in each one with a knot. Then lay the framework on a piece of an old sheet, and cut out a section of sheet about one inch larger all round than the framework. Lap this extra inch round the wire so that the material is stretched fairly tightly and evenly over the framework, and sew it on.

Tie pieces of string about fifteen inches long to the four, six and eight o'clock struts; join the ends together and add a yard of extra string on which scraps of coloured paper have been knotted every few inches. Then, from the centre and from the ten, twelve, and two o'clock struts, run four more short lengths of string, joined at their ends. To this join is tied the end of the kite-string, which should be rolled on a stick when not in use.

Building a Rabbit Hutch

Much of the wood for this can be salvaged scraps, such as pieces of old orange crates. To keep rabbits warm and dry they should be well off the ground, so you need two posts five feet in length as legs for the front, and two posts four feet in length for the back. Three feet off the ground, mount a four-foot length to join the two front legs and another four-foot length to join the two back legs, and do the same

221

at the top of each pair of legs. You now have two frames. These are joined at the three-foot level by two pieces three feet in length, and at the top by slightly longer pieces because there is a slope from front to back to allow water to run off the roof.

Fasten boards across the framework of the floor to cover it, and also cover the back, sides and roof, allowing an overhang at the front to keep the rain off. Then, inside, mount a division two-thirds of the way along, with a hole in it about eight by six inches square to allow easy movement from the larger day-section to the sleeping-area. If two strips of wood are mounted on each side of this doorway, a sliding door can then be fitted which is raised or lowered by a string from outside the hutch.

The front of the hutch is simply two doors, one being a wooden frame with netting attached for the day-section; the other, for the sleeping-area, is built up of boards attached to two cross-pieces on the inside, and with half a dozen holes half an inch in diameter bored through to provide ventilation.

A piece of roofing-felt, tacked on to the roof and lapped over the edges, completes the job. If you use creosote or paint to protect it from the weather, be sure to give the hutch a few days to dry out thoroughly before putting it into use.

Building a Dog Kennel

If your dog has to sleep out of doors then he needs a warm and comfortable kennel. This need not be expensive if you make it of second-hand floor-boards, of which your local wood-yard or buillding contractor is almost certain to have a supply. For the average-size dog, a kennel three feet by two feet in area is sufficient. The floor of this is made by cutting enough boards three feet in length and joining them underneath by nailing across two strong pieces of timber, each two feet long. The sides, three feet long and two feet

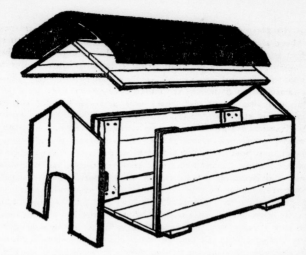

six inches in height, are built up in the same way, with the cross-pieces nailed on the inside. The back has a width of two feet two inches (if your floor-boards are each an inch thick), and is three feet three inches in height. Mark the top centre, then two points two feet six inches from the base at each side; rule lines from the side marks to the top centre, and cut away to make an inverted 'V' shape. Do the same at the front, allowing for an entrance two feet high and twelve inches wide. Across the inside of the top of this doorway you will need a cross-piece, if your timbers run vertically. If they run horizontally, you will need a vertical cross-piece at each side.

The two sections of the roof are each three feet four inches by eighteen inches, to leave an overhang at the front and sides. The roof will need a covering of roofing-felt, lapped over its edges, to keep out the damp. The whole of the sides and back can be covered in the same way to keep out draughts.

Collecting as a Hobby

Stamp Collecting

Of all the hobbies there are, probably none has such widespread popularity as stamp collecting. Mililons of people in the world today are, have been, or will be, stamp collectors.

The first postage stamps were issued in Britain, in 1840, to overcome the problem of standardising postal rates, which had become so high that most ordinary folk couldn't afford to send letters. The first country to follow Britain's lead was Brazil, in 1843, and by 1870 most of the principal nations had adopted the idea of stamps to pay postal charges. By that time the practice of collecting these stamps was firmly established. In those days, and indeed until twenty or thirty years ago, it was still possible to make a serious attempt to collect the stamps of all countries, but nowadays most 'philatelists' prefer to specialise. Here are a few suggestions for collections with plenty of scope yet which are reasonable enough in size to ensure that an active collector is not fighting a losing battle and collecting stamps more slowly than new ones are being issued:

Australasia
British Commonwealth Africa
British Commonwealth America
Great Britain, Cyprus, Gibraltar
    and Malta
British Commonwealth Asia
France and Colonies
Spain and Portugal, with their Colonies
North America
South America
The Caribbean
China and Japan

All of these are groups on which you can make a good start, by using parts of a general collection which has grown out of hand. But if you are really ambitious, you might like to choose 'thematics'—the modern idea of collecting stamps by subject rather than by countries. This way you can make a collection which will serve as an aid to your other interests and hobbies. The following are subjects on which enough stamps have been issued to make any one of them suitable for a large collection:

> The history of aviation
> The sea and shipping
> World transport
> Engineering
> Botany
> Birds, animals and fishes
> World sport
> Exploration
> Scouting, and other youth movements

But in making a choice what could be better than inventing your own theme—an original one which you can feel sure will make yours the only collection of its kind?

Collecting Match-box Labels

Collecting match-box labels, like stamp collecting, is a hobby dating back to the last century. You set about it by saving all you can find and making exchanges with other collectors for the ones you need.

Remove the labels from the boxes by soaking them for a few minutes in hot water, peeling them off, and then drying them between sheets of blotting paper. Loose-leaf albums are the best for mounting collections, and stamp-hinges will safely fix them to the page.

British match-box labels are usually rather dull and uninteresting in design, but there are thousands of foreign ones with highly-coloured action pictures on them. You can find labels showing portraits of native warriors, ships and planes, railways, and you can find some with exciting forgeries printed by wartime resistance groups, bearing slogans encouraging the guerrilla fighters.

Coin Collecting

This is a hobby in which the lucky collector can still come across rare finds of great value or tremendous historical interest. Unlike stamps and match-box labels, coins can be lost for centuries and still survive undamaged, and it is not unusual, when new ground is being turned over or old buildings are being demolished, for coins dating back even as far as Roman times to be unearthed. Coins have been in existence since about 700 B.C., and appeared in Britain before the last century B.C.

Modern coins of many countries can be obtained easily through exchange or by buying a bag of assorted foreign coins.

A cabinet to house your collection needs shallow drawers lined with baize into which holes have been cut to let the coins lie snugly without moving. A small gummed identification label can be stuck below each coin.

Cigarette-card Collecting

Cigarette manufacturers no longer issue cards in their packets, but for many years, until 1939, there was a card in nearly every packet in Britain, the Commonwealth and many other countries. Millions of these have survived, and so it is still possible to start collecting. But the wise collector will look beyond cigarette cards to include *all* cards of a similar kind—which means the many issued in packets and boxes of tea and sweets. Sets, usually of twenty-five or fifty, range in subject from great sportsmen to ocean fishes, from ancient weapons to Derby winners. Many cards issued in the ten years before World War II were accompanied by albums for mounting them.

Older relatives may be able to add to your collection, and cards may also be purchased from dealers.

Cheese-label Collecting

The proper name for this is 'fromology', and the makers of cheese in many countries have recognised the rapid growth of the hobby in recent years by issuing many new and colourful designs. It is possible to build up a collection of more than thirty thousand different labels by exchanging with other collectors. The original source of supply is, of course, your own family kitchen. Friends travelling abroad and pen pals in foreign countries can help to enlarge your collection.

A collection of cheese labels is best mounted and stored in the same way as a stamp collection, using stamp-hinges to fasten the labels in place in a safe way so that they can be removed for exchange or remounting without damage. Removing labels which are gummed tightly to the wrapping of the cheese is best done without using water, as certain labels have colours which 'run' when moistened. Suitable methods are levering the label off the paper by cautious work with a paper knife or peeling off one corner and allowing steam from a kettle to penetrate the glue without coming into direct contact with the printed surface.

There are plenty of different pictorial subjects on cheese labels, ranging from wild animals, flowers and country scenes to aircraft, ships and sportsmen.

Collecting Old Books

This is a hobby for those who enjoy reading and who are, perhaps, interested in writing as well. And though buying new books is expensive, collecting old ones is a hobby that, if carried out carefully, need cost no more than a few pence a week.

Your own interests and other hobbies will help you to decide the subjects which will form the basis of your collection. There are, of course, hundreds to choose from, but a few which can make absorbingly interesting collections without much cost are:

Printing—its history and development
Your favourite sport
What towns and countries looked like in the past
Early cars and railways
Wild life at home and abroad

These suggestions have been made bearing in mind the available sources of old books—second-hand book shops, junk shops and auction rooms. Very often at small auctions you can buy odd lots of books fifty or a hundred years old for prices as low as fifty pence for a hundred. Of this hundred, ninety-five are likely to be completely useless to you, but exchanges with other collectors, or even subsequent auctions, will enable you to get rid of the ones you don't want.

Condition is important if you are collecting books for their own sake, but if you are simply hoping, for instance, to accumulate pictures and information about early railways, you will not be unduly worried if some of your books have torn covers and missing pages. Damaged books can be repaired quite easily (see *Bookbinding*, page 219) so your bookcases need not remain untidy simply because your books, when you bought them, were in shabby condition.

Collecting Pottery

Collectors of rare china pay thousands of pounds for individual pieces of particular quality and historical interest, but you can have just as much fun for a few pence and build up a collection with as much variety. Auction rooms and junk shops have large quantities of old china and pottery which change hands for very low prices, and though much of it is rubbish, now and again rare and attractive oddments can be found among the heaps of old teacups and pie-dishes. But if this doesn't appeal to you then the collecting of modern pottery may. In Britain, and in many other countries, there are small 'one-man' potteries producing excellent craftsmanship. If you buy their work at fashionable shops you will have to pay high prices for it, but if on holiday in Devon and Cornwall for example, you visit some of these tiny potteries, you can buy the same articles for a considerably lower price.

Keeping Pets

Dogs

Choosing a dog for a pet needs careful thought. It isn't enough to decide, 'That's for me!' when a friendly puppy in a pet shop rolls his eyes at you and licks your hand. What you have to consider is the size he will reach, the amount of exercise he'll need, and the amount he is likely to eat. You also have to make up your mind whether the desire to have a dog is just a passing fancy or a feeling that will remain, for when you have bought or been given a dog not only does that dog belong to you, *but you belong to him*. Dogs have as intense a feeling of loyalty as do human beings, and an unwanted dog feels just as lost as an unwanted person does.

There are many breeds from which to choose a dog that suits your requirements; or you may prefer a mongrel to a pedigree pup. Your local dogs' home will be able to help you there. Remember that a large dog can be an encumbrance in a flat or a small house—and his food bills will be high. A dog bred for an active open-air life may be unhappy in a town. So think it over carefully before making your choice.

As soon as you get your dog, buy him a licence if he is over six months old. This can be obtained at any Post Office. It is against the law to keep a dog without a licence.

He will need a box or basket. Dog baskets are rather expensive, but a comfortable box can be made out of scrap wood without any difficult carpentry. Make it big enough for him to move about in and to stretch in his sleep, yet cosy enough to keep him warm. The box should be in a corner free from draughts, and should be lined with several newspapers to keep in the warmth. On top of these he should have an old rug or blanket, or, alternatively, an old eiderdown. Don't just give him a pillow; most dogs like to roll themselves up in their bedding, just as many of us do. The bedding should be taken out of doors and shaken every day or two and the newspaper changed at frequent intervals.

If you have a garden and your dog is able to get plenty of exercise in it, then one short walk every day should be all he needs. Except in country districts, this should preferably be on a lead.

He will probably be untrained when you first get him. Training needs patience, and if it seems to take a long time, remember that the training of a human baby takes far longer. It will help your puppy if you can start off with a regular routine of meals, walks and grooming.

At first, puppies need to be let out of doors every two or three hours during the day. A few messes indoors must be expected, and the dog which learns quickly is the one which is praised for attending to his needs out of doors rather than the one which is punished for making a mess in the hall.

Teach your dog to 'come to heel' when taken out of doors without a lead. A little perseverance should make him completely obedient to your orders. A disobedient dog is less to blame than his owner, for a dog naturally regards man as his master and disobeys only when that master no longer deserves respect. To earn that respect, you have to be absolutely consistent about discipline. If your dog is punished or spoken to sharply for making a mess on the pavements then he must *always* be punished or spoken to sharply for it. If he is praised when he comes to heel promptly, then he must *always* be praised. Above all, he must never be punished without knowing why.

Grooming needs vary for different breeds of dogs. Short-haired dogs need only a brisk rub-down from time to time with a rough towel or a brush; long-haired varieties need more frequent attention, with a steel comb and stiff brush. Your dog should be taught to look forward to this as a regular habit and should be complimented on his smartness afterwards. Washing need not be frequent for most breeds and should be done either with ordinary toilet soap or with dog soap sold by your pet-shop. Don't use kitchen soap, as the soda will harm his coat as well as irritate the pores of his skin. The temperature of the water should be moderate. Immediately after his bath your dog should be very thoroughly dried, otherwise he'll undertake this himself and in doing so probably make himself dirtier than he was before.

A dog's diet should consist of about a half ounce of meat for each pound of his weight, as well as about the same amount of cereal and vegetable matter. The quantities required must be adjusted according to the amount of exercise the dog gets. It is as important not to over-feed as it is not to under-feed, as over-feeding brings about various stomach troubles which may be difficult to cure.

Meat should not be overcooked, and many dogs prefer it raw. Bones, carefully chosen in order to avoid those which may cause injury through sharp splinters, are used by most dogs more as playthings than as a source of food, and to compensate a dog for the lack of mineral from bones he should be given a small amount of ground bone-meal in his diet.

A puppy should be fed four or five times a day, but by the time a dog is fully grown he should be fed only one main meal a day and should know the exact time at which to expect his food. Your dog should always have access to a supply of fresh water.

Cats

A kitten is ready to leave its mother at eight weeks, by which time it should have learned to attend to its needs out of doors or in an ash-box placed in a corner. A cat needs the same kind of bedding as a dog, also the same chance to go out of doors for exercise. Do not attempt to

232

help a cat keep itself clean; unlike dogs, cats spend much of their time doing this very efficiently, and your assistance will not be appreciated.

Kittens should receive several feeds a day, but by the time they are six months old this should have been reduced to two, or even one, given at regular times of the day. A healthy adult cat should receive about half an ounce of food for every pound it weighs. Milk, meat, fish, liver, and most table scraps, providing they do not contain too much spice, are their basic diet. A cat should always have access to a supply of fresh water.

Mice

All varieties of tame mice need a warm temperature, and must be given a cage with plenty of room. Its floor should be littered with clean sawdust, which should be changed frequently. Grain mixture and bread is the ideal diet, with fragments of cheese and greenstuff. The water supply must be kept fresh.

Hamsters

Golden hamsters are kept in the same way as mice. As well as bread and cereal, they enjoy carrots, maize meal and milk.

Guinea-pigs

Guinea-pigs are best kept out of doors in a warm shed which is thoroughly proofed against rats, cats and dogs. They should have an outdoor run on the sheltered side of their shed. The shed itself should contain plenty of litter for bedding; wood-wool or fine shavings are ideally suitable for this. The bedding should be changed frequently to avoid unpleasant smells and the danger of disease. Guinea-pigs need about an ounce of cereal daily (bran and crushed oats), with a plentiful supply of garden greenstuff. Fresh water should always be available.

Rabbits

Rabbits require much the same housing as guinea-pigs but the food may be more varied. Rabbits will thrive on many kinds of household scraps, such as bread, cooked potatoes and plenty of green food.

Tortoises

A tortoise, as he carries his own house with him, needs only a shelter to keep off heavy rain and wind. A small wooden box on its side in the garden is adequate. In a garden which contains plants of value it may be necessary to limit the tortoise's movements by boards or low fencing, for he will spend much of his time wandering about and sampling different kinds of greenstuff. In winter he will hibernate, and it is important to know *where,* as once this has happened he must not be disturbed until the warmer weather returns. If brought into a greenhouse or shed to hibernate in a box, he should be given plenty of straw and dry leaves with which to cover himself completely. If he hibernates in the garden, he will probably fail to cover himself with a thick enough layer of earth to keep out the frost, and so a thick wad of straw should be placed on top.

During the summer the moisture from greenstuff may be insufficient; a tortoise should then be given a supply of fresh water in a shallow plate or saucer.

Cage Birds

Canaries require a diet composed of canary seed, summer rape seed, cuttlefish bone and a little greenstuff. Fresh water should always be provided in the cage. Budgerigars should receive millet and canary seed, with lettuce or other greenstuff in small quantities. The secret of successful bird-keeping is attention to cleanliness; the cage must be kept spotlessly clean and the water changed as often as possible. Care must also be taken to prevent draughts.

Easy-to-Grow Flowers

If starting a small corner of your own in the family garden, prepare the ground by digging over thoroughly and removing weeds and grass. Work in any compost or old manure before planting. Here are some flowers which are easy to grow, some of which you might like to try in your own garden. (Remember, annuals are plants which last only a single year; biennials flower in their second year and then die; perennials live on from year to year.)

Ageratum is a half-hardy annual, with mauve, pink, blue or white flowers, 6 to 9 inches in height. It is sown under glass in early spring.

Alyssum is a useful hardy annual for sunny borders and rockeries. It can be sown in the open and has mauve or white flowers. Perennial varieties are also available. Height 3 to 6 inches.

Antirrhinum, usually known as *Snapdragon*, can be grown as an annual or kept as a perennial. It is sown under glass from January to March and planted out in May. Height ranges from 6 inches to 3 feet; all colours are available except blue.

Armeria, also called *Thrift*, is a cushiony, hardy perennial with red, pink or white flowers, ideal for borders and rockeries. Height 6 inches.

Aster, a family of half-hardy annuals available in many colours, includes the *Michaelmas Daisy*—a hardy perennial which ranges from blue and mauve to pale pink and white. *China Asters*, sown in May, are ideal as cut flowers.

Aubrietia is a trailing rock-plant (hardy perennial) with purple or pink flowers. It is best grown from cuttings.

Calendula, or *Pot Marigold,* a half-hardy annual with double or single flowers, ranges from pale yellow to a rich gold. Sown in early spring, it should provide plenty of colour in late summer. Height 18 to 30 inches.

Candytuft is grown from seed as a hardy annual or perennial. The average height is 12 inches; the spiked flowers are pink, crimson or lilac.

Cheiranthus, or *Siberian Wallflower,* is available in yellow and orange. Sown in May and transplanted after reaching a height of 2 inches, it flowers the following year. Height 18 inches.

Chrysanthemums are of two kinds. The hardy annuals are sown in the open in spring for summer flowering; the perennials can be grown from cuttings and root division. There are many varieties and shades, and chrysanthemums are the mainstay of the autumn flower-bed. Height 18 inches to 3 feet.

Clarkia is a hardy annual with pastel or white flowers. It is sown in April and grows to about 24 inches in height.

Cornflower, a hardy annual, is easy to grow and has a wide range of colours. Height 2 to 2½ feet.

Crocus is a hardy perennial, yellow, white or purple, with a corm or bulb which is planted in the early autumn for flowering the following spring.

Dahlia is a half-hardy perennial with a tuberous root. It can be raised from seed, and after flowering the tubers can be stored away from frost for replanting the next year. It comes in a variety of colours, and varies in size from 18 inches to 5 feet.

Delphinium is of two varieties. The annual, known as *Larkspur,* is planted as seed in the spring; the perennial is often raised from cuttings planted in spring or autumn. It is usually available in various shades of blue and is from 2 to 6 feet in height.

236

Dianthus is the family which includes the *Carnation, Pink* and *Sweet William*. Hardy border carnations are propagated by cutting, and so are pinks. Sweet Williams are grown from seed as biennials.

Gladiolus is a tall flowering plant grown from a corm planted in the spring. In early autumn the corms are lifted and the new offset corms removed and stored to start fresh plants the next spring. The plant grows from 30 inches to 4½ feet in height and is available in a wide variety of colours.

Gypsophila is a pink or white annual, grown from seed in March. A perennial variety can be raised from root division. Height about 18 inches.

Hyacinth is a bulb planted in October for spring flowering, or in pots indoors from August onwards for mid-winter. Available in many colours, it grows to about 12 inches in height.

Iris is a hardy perennial with roots that divide easily for propagation in the late autumn. It is available in a great variety of heights and colours.

Lobelia is best started under glass in early spring. The mass of blue or white flowers it produces is ideal for borders and rockeries.

Love-in-a-Mist is an annual with blue or white flowers, and is sown in the open in March or April. Height 18 inches.

Narcissus is a class of bulb which includes the *Daffodil*. It is planted in the late summer or early autumn for spring flowering, and need not be lifted except when so many new bulbs have formed that splitting becomes necessary.

Nasturtium is sown in the open as soon as the danger of frost is past. There are many varieties, ranging from pale yellow to deep orange in colour.

Phlox is a hardy annual or perennial available in a variety of colours. The annual is sown under glass in spring for summer flowering; the perennial is best increased by cuttings in early spring or October. Height from 1 to 5 feet.

Primula is a member of the family which includes *Primroses* and *Polyanthus*. All varieties can be raised from seed, but the usual method is by splitting old plants after flowering has ended.

Roses are best planted in early November. There are a number of types, such as ramblers, bushes and standards, climbers and polyanthus. Most varieties need pruning for good results. In general, the rule is that strong growers are lightly pruned and weak growers need more severe treatment.

Sweet Pea is a hardy annual grown mainly for cut flowers. Sown in autumn or spring, it requires good, well-manured soil. The more sweet peas are picked, the more they flower. The range of colours and sizes is considerable.

Tulip is a hardy perennial bulb plant for early spring flowering. It is planted in autumn in the open. It can also be grown indoors in pots.

Garden Calendar

January. Take cuttings of chrysanthemums from the bases of old plants and set them in pots containing leaf-mould and old mortar. Sow sweet peas in boxes under glass.

February. Plant onions, leeks, shallots and early peas in the open. Sow spinach, parsnips and early carrots if the ground is not frozen.

March. Plant broccoli, Brussels sprouts, cabbage, carrots, cauliflower, lettuce, peas, potatoes, parsley, radishes and summer cabbages In the open. Plant pinks and carnations, and begin sowing annuals.

April. Plant French beans, cauliflower, beetroot, celery, lettuce, mustard and cress, peas, potatoes, spinach, summer turnips and marrows. Sow remaining annuals, and plant shrubs.

May. Plant further crops of potatoes, lettuce and cabbage. Sow runner beans, further annuals, also sweet williams, wallflowers, forget-me-nots and Canterbury bells. Plant early chrysanthemums.

June. Plant tomatoes, sweet corn and cucumber. Plant dahlia tubers and hardy perennials.

July. Plant out winter cabbages. Sow further annuals for autumn flowering, and plant out biennials sown in May.

August. Sow winter spinach, winter swedes and turnips in the open. Plant crocuses, narcissi and snowdrops, as well as bulbs in fibre for indoor display.

September. Continue sowing winter vegetables. Harvest root crops and gather tomatoes. Plant irises and additional narcissi and crocuses.

October. Plant spring cabbages. Lift dahlias and gladioli. Prepare soil for roses.

November. Sow broad beans. Plant and transplant trees and shrubs. Plant cuttings from perennials and also increase them by root-splitting. Plant roses.

December. Start of the best season for digging. Remove weeds. Prepare trenches for sweet peas. Take chrysanthemum cuttings.

Judging the Weather

The following is a rough guide to judging the weather by means of a household barometer.
1. If the needle or mercury is rising, calm or fair weather can be expected.
2. If the needle or mercury is falling, expect rain and unsettled weather.
3. A rising and falling barometer indicates changeable weather.
4. A steady barometer means that the weather is likely to continue as at the time of reading.
5. A very slow rise or fall indicates the approach of a good or bad settled condition.

Indoor Games

Indoor games can be excellent fun, especially as your skill in mastering them increases. Here are the rules of a few of the standard games:

Chess

The game is for two players, each of whom has sixteen playing pieces. One set is white, the other either red or black. A board of sixty-four black and white squares in eight rows of eight is used, turned so that each player has a white square in the right-hand corner nearest him.

White always starts the game, and the players toss to decide which of them shall have the white pieces. The purpose of the game is to capture the opponent's King.

White sets up his men on the two rows nearest him: back row (1. to r.) — Castle, Knight, Bishop, Queen, King, Bishop, Knight, Castle; second row - the Pawns. Black puts each of his men exactly opposite White's.

Each player has (in order of importance): a King and a Queen; two Castles; two Knights; two Bishops; eight Pawns. These can make the following moves:

King: one square at a time in any direction (so long as the square is empty).

Queen: as many unoccupied squares as desired, in any direction and either diagonally or straight.

Bishops: diagonally, in either direction, as many unoccupied squares as desired.

Knights: one square straight, then one diagonally, regardless of intervening pieces (provided a Knight does not finish on a square holding one of its own men).

Castles: straight, in either direction, as many squares as desired.

Pawns: one square forward, except in their first move, which may be two squares if wished, and in 'capturing', when they move one forward and one to left or right.

It does not matter how many pieces you lose in capturing your opponent's King. This is done by placing him in 'check'—a position in which he could be captured at the next move. He must then move out of check, and if unable to do so he is 'check-mated', and thus defeated. The game can end in a 'stalemate', or draw, when a player's King, though not in check, is unable to move without moving into check and the player has no other piece to move. The game may also be drawn when neither player can capture the other's King.

Once in any game a player may 'castle'. If neither the King nor the Castle in question has moved so far, and the King is nor in check, the King may move two squares towards the Castle, which is then placed on the last square passed over by the King. The purpose of this is to move the King to greater safety and at the same time to bring the Castle into play. You cannot castle if your King is in check or if opposing pieces are in the way.

A Pawn reaching the eighth line may be exchanged for any other piece.

Draughts

This is played on the black squares of a chess-board, using two sets of men, each consisting of twelve black and twelve red or white circular pieces. These are arranged on the black squares of the first three rows at each end of the board, and move one square forward, diagonally. The purpose of the game is to capture all the opponent's pieces, which is done by jumping across them to a vacant square beyond. If, by so doing, the attacker then lands on a square from which it is able to capture again, it does so without waiting for the next move. On reaching the opponent's back line, a piece becomes a King by having a captured piece placed on top, and thenceforward may move forward or back.

Any piece in a position to make a capture but which does not do so is 'huffed'—removed from play.

Marbles

There are several varieties of this game, the best known being Ring Taw, in which one player places his marbles in a circle and the other flicks his in turn towards them from a distance of six feet. A hit wins the marble.

Secret Codes

The simplest secret codes are made by merely advancing every letter of every word by two, three or four in the alphabet; thus, using a four-stage code, the word 'alphabet' would become 'eptlefix'. Rapid coding and decoding of messages using this system can be done by drawing a large circle and writing the alphabet round it, leaving equal distances between each letter. A smaller circle is cut out of a sheet of paper, and the alphabet written once more round it. This is pinned to the centre of the larger circle, so that it can be rotated. Move it four stages forward, and every letter is moved by the same amount.

But this kind of code can be solved very easily, and for messages of top secrecy a more complicated code can be made with very little trouble. Both the sender and receiver of the code message must agree in advance upon a secret code word. It can be any word as long as no letter occurs more than once. Let's say, for example, that it is the word 'DIVER'.

Draw a square and divide it into twenty-five small squares. Starting at the top left-hand corner, fill in the letters of the code word, one in each square, and then the remaining letters of the alphabet in correct order, omitting the ones used already and also omitting 'J', because as we have only twenty-five squares the same code symbol has to serve for both 'I' and 'J'.

The method of coding and decoding may at first seem rather complicated, but a little practise will enable you to carry it out rapidly. Begin by dividing your message into pairs of letters. Thus 'DO NOT RETURN TO BASE' would become 'DO NO TR ET UR NT OB AS EQ'.

The letter 'Q' is added as a dummy to complete the final, pair.

Now your code square, with 'DIVER' as its code word, looks like this:

D	I	V	E	R
A	B	C	F	G
H	K	L	M	N
O	P	Q	S	T
U	W	X	Y	Z

Looking at your pairs of letters waiting for coding, you can see that any two letters are either on the same vertical line, such as 'DO', on the same horizontal line, or at opposite corners of a square or rectangle. If the letters are in the same vertical column, each is translated into code by using the next letter above it, the very top letter of a column being coded by the one at the bottom. Thus 'DO' becomes 'UH' in code. A group on the same horizontal line is coded by using for each letter the one immediately on its right, with the end right-hand letter coded by the one at the extreme left. Letters at opposite corners of a square or rectangle are coded by taking the letters at the other corners of the square or rectangle, so that 'NO' becomes 'HT', and 'ET' becomes 'RS'. The original message, 'DO NOT RETURN TO BASE', becomes, in code, 'UH HT NZ RS ZD GN PA FO VS'. To decode this when receiving at the other end, you simply work the whole process in reverse, using a similar code square. The only other factor to be remembered is that it is impossible to code a pair of identical letters, such as 'BB' or 'OO', for obvious reasons, and it is necessary, therefore, to put a 'Q' between them while dividing the message into groups.

There are many other codes in use, but though some of them are very much more complicated, nearly all of them depend upon the principle used in this twenty-five-square system.

244

Personal Record

The following section is about *you*. We've dealt with facts and figures on hundreds of subjects of world-wide importance; now what about yourself? Where do *you* fit in, and what kind of person are you? Here, then, is the personal record which not only reminds you of facts and figures which may otherwise get lost or forgotten but helps you to find out more about yourself.

Full Name :
Date of Birth :
Address :
Telephone Number :
School :   *School Number :*
Savings Book Number :
Club Number :
Medical Card Number :
Position in School :

Term	*Year*	*Class*	*Position*
Spring	19		
Summer	19		
Autumn	19		
Spring	19		
Summer	19		
Autumn	19		
Spring	19		
Summer	19		
Autumn	19		

Weight and Height Charts

These two graphs will help you to note your own progress. As you fill in the dots marking your height and weight at different ages, link them up to form a line from the bottom left corner to the top right of each graph.

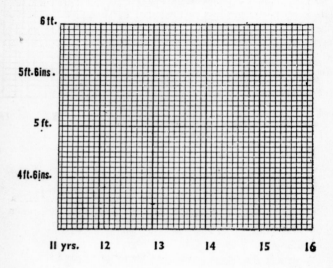

Height

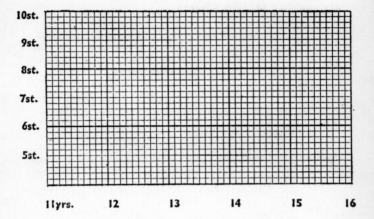

Weight

Athletics Charts

If you want to find out whether you're above or below average in field and track events, try comparing your own performances with this set of standards.

Average Performances for Boys of 12 to 13

Event	Average Performance		
100 yards	12.8 s.	to	13.4 s.
220 yards	29 s.	to	32 s.
70 yards hurdles	12.5 s.	to	13.5 s.
4 by 110 yards relay	57 s.	to	60 s.
Long jump	13 ft.	to	13 ft. 6 in.
High jump	3 ft. 10 in.	to	4 ft. 1 in.

Average Performances for Boys of 13 to 14

Event	Average Performance		
100 yards	12.6 s.	to	13 s.
220 yards	29 s.	to	31 s.
440 yards	67 s.	to	74 s.
880 yards	2 m. 40 s.	to	2 m. 50 s.
75 yards hurdles	12.9 s.	to	13.4 s.
80 yards hurdles	13.1 s.	to	13.6 s.
4 by 110 yards relay	54 s.	to	57 s.
Long jump	13 ft. 8 in.	to	14 ft. 3 in.
High jump	4 ft.	to	4 ft. 3 in.
Discus	roughly		70 ft.
Javelin	roughly		70 ft.
Shot putt	roughly		20 ft.

Average Performances for Boys of 14 to 15

Event	Average Performance		
100 yards	12.3 s.	to	12.7 s.
220 yards	18 s.	to	30 s.
440 yards	65 s.	to	70 s.
880 yards	2 m. 28 s.	to	2 m. 35 s
75 yards hurdles	12.8 s.	to	13.5 s.
80 yards	13 s.	to	13.8 s.
4 by 110 yards relay	52 s.	to	55 s.
Long jump	14 ft. 9 in.	to	15 ft. 1 in.
High jump	4 ft. 3 in.	to	4 ft. 6 in.
Discus	roughly		90 ft.
Javelin	roughly		95 ft.
Shot putt	roughly		30 ft.

Average Performances for Boys of 15 to 16

Event	Average Performance		
100 yards	11.3 s.	to	12 s.
220 yards	26 s.	to	29 s.
440 yards	61 s.	to	68 s.
880 yards	2 m. 24 s.	to	2 m. 31 s.
110 yards hurdles	16 s.	to	19 s.
Long jump	14 ft. 11 in.	to	15 ft. 9 in.
High jump	4 ft. 6 in.	to	4 ft. 9 in.
Discus	roughly		98 ft.
Javelin	roughly		100 ft.
Shot putt	roughly		35 ft.

Charts such as the ones on the following pages show you how to keep records of your own best performances each season, and lines drawn to join each entry to the next will reveal how steady your improvement is.

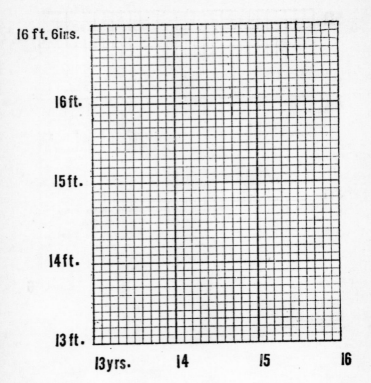

Long Jump

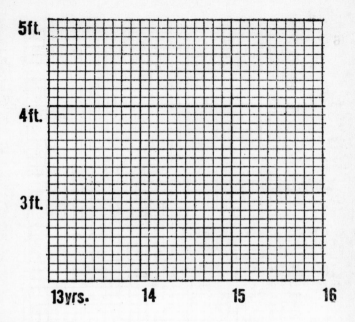

High Jump

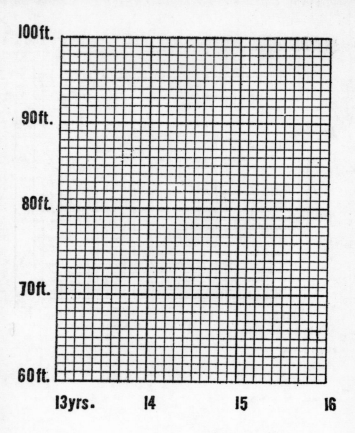

Discus

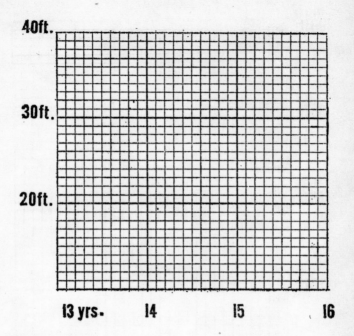

40ft.

30ft.

20ft.

13 yrs.   **14**   **15**   **16**

Shot Putt

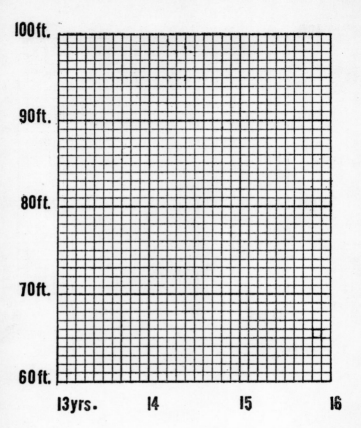

Javelin